BETTER EVERY DAY

SUSANA MONTUORI

CONTENTS

INTRODUCTION

Hazel eyes follow my hand as it trails along the wires of the cage. The metal reverberates as my fingers ripple gently across the chain links. I glide my hand slowly at first, then faster, back and forth, back and forth. He fixates on the motion.

"Hey," I say, a half-hearted effort to distract him.

No reaction. His eyes remain steady. Carefully he gathers his legs underneath his massive body. It seems impossible to stand without moving one's head, but he does. He is taller than me now as I balance precariously on one knee. A thin line of saliva dangles from his mouth. His stance, a bit unnerving, offers no real threat, intimidation securely tempered by the wire between us.

I run my hand up the cage, then down. His bulky head lowers. One fuzzy front foot rises in slow motion then stops, suspended in the air. The eyes never lose contact. I move my head closer. We are inches apart.

"Hey," I say again, almost a whisper this time.

Nothing.

I hold my breath. My hand is still. We are still. Three seconds, four. He stares. I stare. Five seconds, six. Statues, the two of us. Seven, eight, which of us will break?

My index finger twitches ever so slightly. And it's over.

In one mighty explosion, he unleashes his attack. Strong haunches propel him forward, shattering the air between us. A mass of fur and teeth fly towards me. Giant front paws land squarely against the wire. The cage rattles with the force.

"Ah!" I yell, losing my balance.

My hands slap against the concrete as I fall backward, legs splayed. One beaded sandal rests beside me, having popped off on impact. The outcome was inevitable. Still, the anticipation was so intense, his action so sudden. Laughing, I right myself from the awkward position and brush off my jeans, scanning for onlookers.

The spell broken, he looks contentedly at me, shakes his enormous head, and sneezes.

1

HEAVEN

Heaven goes by favor. If it went by merit, you would stay
out and your dog would go in. – Mark Twain

IF I WERE AS PERFECT a creature as a dog, heaven would
certainly be my destiny. Alas, I cannot recall a day that I have
been even the slightest bit worthy of the blessing. On this
steamy Saturday, I find myself surrounded by those angelic
creatures, as near to their benevolent nature as I'll ever be.

I am at our local animal shelter, temporary home to
wayward souls arriving under different circumstances,
hoping for a better outcome. Animal rescue facilities and
their philanthropic-minded supporters are abundant
throughout the east coast of southern Florida. There are four
in my neighborhood. This one is ten minutes from my house.
I pass it daily during my commute but never take time to stop.
Today I take the time, kneeling before the cages, sticking my
fingers through the wires to touch the dogs that will come

close enough to inspect my hand or let me scratch behind their ears.

It is early, though the thunder of cars on the nearby highway would say otherwise. Humidity thickens the air. The heat index is rising. *Eighty-six degrees with an expected high of ninety-two,* my car radio had blared only minutes earlier. Typical for south Florida during the summer, the weatherman had covered the warning signs of heat stroke, cautioning children and the elderly in particular. I am not elderly, nor am I a child. I'm not even sweating. I am exactly where I want to be—sitting on the cool cement floor of a smelly, old, cinder block building, surrounded by dogs.

Lately, I've felt an essential part of me was missing; the part that makes breathing and living a little less overwhelming—I was without a dog. I hold a particular fondness for dogs—an affliction inherited from my father. A quiet and distant man who held a deep respect for his animals, my father's dogs were his passion. I made his passion mine. Growing up, I connected with animals much easier than I did with people. My childhood had included a lively Chesapeake Bay, a maternal Newfoundland, a pair of enormous Labradors who believed they were lap dogs, several stubborn terriers, and a tenacious Border Collie. They were my security blankets, snuggling close when I was tired or scared, my playmates when I was lonely, and my partners on youthful adventures.

The ancient air conditioning system whistles and wheezes, blowing cool air on my neck, inviting me to stay a while longer. Positioned on the floor in front of one cage, I inhale a slow breath and let it out. With my legs crossed in front of me, I appear to be meditating at some retreat, though my surroundings lack a serene atmosphere. Every bark and howl echoes against the cinder block walls. Stainless steel doors squeak and rattle as morning volunteers let dogs in and out. A rush of thunderous barking ensues as each dog passes by the others on their way to the exercise yard. Two rows of kennels span the length of the building, twenty-two individual enclosures in each row. The walkways in between are still damp from a morning spray, intensifying the putrid odor of urine and feces, now mixed with an antiseptic smell.

The animal shelter is an unusual place to find calm perhaps, and yet for me, time lingers—a brief pause between the more pressing needs in my life. I close my eyes and take it in, ingesting it like water on the hot summer day. Being with the animals soothes me.

There are so many dogs to consider—gentle, trusting souls, deliriously happy to see me, their tails furiously wagging their bodies, and the suspicious ones, who gaze at me and refuse to come close, protected by the wires between us. To them, I extend only my quiet presence and soft words.

People can be cruel, I explain telepathically to one shaking soul in the far corner of his cage. *After a while, you don't know whom to trust, so you just avoid them all.* Clearly, he has already come to this conclusion, but I let him know I understand. Though my thoughts are directed toward the dog, I regularly apply this mantra to myself.

Cautious and quiet by nature, I rarely reach out to others. When I do, I pick the wrong ones. If I were to be entirely honest, I welcome questionable people into my life and then use the inevitable outcome as an excuse to retreat. Avoidance is a protective blanket I rarely remove. Living with minimal human interaction is easy for me.

Observing a graying beagle as he sleeps soundly, I shift my position. My thoughts drift to a book I read, a beautiful memoir by a woman who walked the Pacific Crest Trail. She made the trek alone. Where she found the time I wasn't certain, but she was young and not yet burdened with life's responsibilities. She hiked the entire trail to clear her mind, to come to terms with past conflicts, to meditate and grow. Accomplishing that feat without another human made sense to me. Serious soul-searching requires solitude. It struck me as inexplicable, though, that she had done it without a dog. Safety, quiet companionship, a natural hunter, even body heat on cold nights—a dog should have been a requirement. Silly girl.

The Saturday chore list in my head has fallen silent for now. I will stay here with the animals and simply be content to feel their presence. Breathe with them. I have no clear plan anyway, and I am not sure exactly what kind of dog I need.

I spend time with a particularly matted mix, poking my fingers through the wires, clearing a path through the thick hair that covers his eyes. Growing impatient with me, he retreats, and I slide my body over to the next kennel—the next dog.

2

THE BEACH

It is 2010, the year I find myself aimlessly stalking the animal shelter, sitting alone on the worn cement, one shoe off, looking as though I'm the one who needs rescuing.

My initial move from Maryland, four years earlier, followed the completion of cancer treatments. A slew of equally serious health problems that hovered over me like a black cloud for several years had lifted, allowing me time to regroup and exhale—if only for a moment. With my health improving and fewer follow-ups needed, I was deemed free to roam by medical professionals. Completely out-of-character, I had taken the opportunity, accepted a job offer, given notice to my boss, packed my young daughter, and myself, and moved to Florida. No more doctors, no more winter coats, no more snow. Best of all, we were at the beach.

Vacationers, I soon realized, were the ones who enjoyed the beach. Residents generally went about their busy lives in the vicinity of the sun and sand. Still, I knew it was there. On my lunch break, I could see the ocean from the eleventh floor of the courthouse where I worked. I could almost feel the ocean breeze as I walked to and from the parking lot. On rare occasions, I detoured down A1A with the windows down, breathing in the salt air and listening to the waves crashing, somewhat muted over the engine of my car, but good enough for me.

My work as a courtroom clerk made relocation an easy adjustment. Courtroom rules of evidence and procedure are historic rituals steeped in tradition and easily transferable from state to state. Years of training and experience allowed for a seamless transition.

The job had always been a good fit. Emotions can run high in a courtroom. Tempers flare. It is my job to remain professionally detached, studiously recording and tracking the proceedings—the proverbial fly-on-the-wall. I have witnessed many a drama while maintaining a meticulous record for posterity. The job is isolating, even in a packed courtroom—which suits me perfectly. Quietly maintaining my distance is what I do best.

In my forties, divorced, and with one child still at home, I had initiated a lot of changes in my life that year, good and bad. On the positive side, I was growing up, finally, and coming to terms with past mistakes and regrets. Then, of course, there was my improving health. On the negative side —there was only one on that list—my son's enlistment in the military. I felt I had initiated that one as well.

While I was moving to warmer weather and new beginnings, my firstborn had been training to fight a war. Charlie seemed to have been fighting a war his whole life, most often with me, but this was different. This was the real thing. Our turbulent relationship had taken an unexpected turn, and suddenly, we were heading in two different directions—his much more ominous.

Even the warm Florida air that first Christmas without Charlie could not remove the chill I felt in my bones. My days were shadowed by a keen awareness of my son's circumstances, and the bumpy path that led him there. But that worry would be with me wherever I was. Maryland, Florida, it didn't matter. Better to try new things—keep myself busy.

So my daughter, Sarah, and I moved and settled into a rented townhouse, then another. Eventually, I surprised myself with the purchase of a run-down property on the outskirts of Palm Beach County. It was an old farmhouse, nine hundred twenty-six square feet. It was basically a closet with running water and in need of a major renovation, but with two bedrooms, two baths and, most importantly, two acres of land—it was perfect. The property was tucked away in a wooded neighborhood just off the main road, private, removed from the world. I liked it for the isolation.

In addition, I appreciated the opportunity to keep animals. Horses had always been a big part of my life, and I was eager to share the experience with my daughter. Immediately, I purchased two. Soon we would have two wooden stalls, a small tack and feed room, and a makeshift riding arena. Typical of those with a passion for horses, improvements to our own living quarters took a back seat to the animals. Horses provide me with the same calming effect as dogs. If only you could bring them into the house.

Over the next four years, with the exception of my job

and Sarah's activities, I rarely ventured farther than the property perimeter. Renovating the house and caring for the animals made my days challenging and busy, which was the point. Short of enlisting to keep an eye on my son, staying busy was the best I could do. It was, really, all I could do.

3

BROWN EYES

TODAY, it is a rare occasion that I have deviated from my usual commute, even rarer that I am sitting still on a Saturday morning observing an array of canine companions. *Just looking*, I remind myself, as though fending off some invisible saleswoman in a clothing store. *Something small and quiet*—though I know it is useless to try to direct the outcome. Dogs usually pick people—if you simply let the process be.

Still, I feel a need to steer the end result to some extent. I love dogs, all dogs, but it is more than that. Certain dogs have centered me, pulled me back from a scattered and crazy world when I couldn't quite manage it myself. A dog with the right temperament can soothe my anxious nature, and I am hoping for *that* dog now, but until the right one stands up and introduces himself, I am content to enjoy them all.

Soon, the attendant appears—a tall high school kid in khakis and sneakers. I ask if I can take a few dogs out to interact with them. He leads them to the exercise area one at a time while the others bark wildly. I spend a little time with each and help him return them to their kennels. The individual attention brightens their day. I silently reaffirm how much it brightens mine.

I glance at a large, mixed breed in one kennel. The attendant asks if I would like to see him. A large dog isn't what I am seeking, but my helper suddenly seems so eager.

"He's a really good dog. Just came in." The young man stands at the door, his hand wavering over the latch. "I can take him out if you want."

"Sure," I respond. Together, we coach the dog out of the kennel. "Why don't you adopt him?" I suggest, sensing he has a personal interest.

The young man looks down at the dog longingly.

"I live with my parents. I can't bring any more animals home. My mom would kill me." He smiles, gently stroking the dog's head.

"Wouldn't she?" he asks the animal, as though they have had this conversation before.

Out in the yard, I watch the dog explore his surroundings, stopping frequently in his travels to inspect me. He's young, maybe one or two years. There is Doberman in his bloodline, but not all—cocoa brown in color, lighter around the muzzle, with broad eyes and floppy ears. Vizsla, possibly? Some Weimaraner, perhaps? Usually, I'm a pretty good judge of mixed breeds, but I'm not entirely sure of this one. He has a sleek body with a deep chest. Long legs bring him slightly above my knee, almost to the middle of my thigh. His tail has not been cropped—the usual practice with Dobermans. Irritated skin covers his ears, neck, and legs. The patches, raw and pink, appear to be dermatitis and not the result of restraint or abuse.

I watch the dog inspect the far corner of the yard. When I call to him, he trots over and sits down, his wide chest spreading out between his forelegs. Even with the dim overhead lighting, I note a distinct absence of male anatomy and, very clearly, two rows of nipples on the dog's underside. He, quite obviously, is a she.

How had the shelter attendant not seen that? Doesn't a vet perform a medical exam upon arrival? My thoughts grow cynical as I consider the competence of the caretakers. Good thing they didn't try to neuter her.

The dog places one paw on my knee, and I take it in my hand. The nails on her foot are worn down to the pads. Rotating her foot slightly in my palm, I note the pads are healing, scarred in some places. Her ribcage protrudes on each side as she sits before me. Clearly, she has been on her own for a while.

"Where have you been?" I whisper as she withdraws her foot and lowers it to the floor.

Deep brown eyes look up at me. Her ears perk, her head tilts to one side and her mouth parts. For a second, I think she might answer. Then, she turns to continue her investigation of the yard, and the moment disintegrates.

Nice dog, I conclude as she glides effortlessly along the fence line, taking huge strides. Not too shy or frightened, not aggressive. She seems inquisitive and rather well-behaved. Keenly aware of my presence, she checks in periodically, as though reassuring herself that I am still here.

The attendant has gone to assist others. The shelter has

become busy. Uncomfortable, now, with too many people in too little space, I am ready to leave.

A family walks by the yard and, as the dog circles around again, I reach for her lead. The parents are arguing loudly. The mother suddenly pushes the father. He pushes back with more force. She bumps hard against the concrete wall, rubbing her arm.

Don't judge, I tell myself, but I am already judging.

"A Doberman!" the smallest boy exclaims. "That's a fightin' dog!"

Two older boys nod in agreement. They stick their fingers through the fence, baring their teeth and growling in an effort to get a reaction. When the dog approaches, one of the boys pokes her in the nose as another tries unsuccessfully to grab her ear. Surprised, she backs away a few steps.

"Let's go," I whisper. She follows me to the gate and sits patiently while I slide the nylon slip around her neck.

Back in her kennel, the dog sighs, circles once and drops down clumsily on the elevated kennel bed—the mat showing the wear of a thousand animals that have rested there before her. I pause to study her one last time. She looks tired, not just physically but like some old soul that carries the weight of the world on her shoulders and could use the temporary respite that the shelter offers. It isn't the ideal place to be, but it is probably better than where she has been.

After latching the gate, I retreat down the line of kennels, fumbling for my car keys. I pass the attendant on my way out. He is talking to the family with the boys—the overly excited, overly loud, overly pokey boys. They are begging their parents for "the Doberman." I note the worry on the attendant's face. As I approach, he meets my eyes.

"This lady was actually looking at him first," he says loudly. "If she decides to take him, then he's not available..." His voice trails off.

I open my mouth to protest, but can't form the words. The entire family turns to stare me down. "The Doberman?" I say. "The brown one?"

I am stalling for time. I have only come to look. Besides, I am considering small dogs, not one as large as her. But what will this dog's fate be at the hands of this family, this arguing, grabbing, pushing family? She is too gentle for them and much too polite.

"Oh, come *on*," one of the boys whines impatiently, rolling his eyes and suddenly making my decision so much easier.

I can't save all of the dogs from them, but this one—

"Oh, yes," I hear myself saying, some stranger commandeering my mouth. "I'm taking the Doberman."

The boys throw a fit, hands in the air, spewing a steady stream of cuss words in my direction. Feeling vindicated and coolly gratified, if a little shocked, I march back towards the animal's cage.

Following the obligatory paper signing, instructions for a free vet exam and payment of the forty-five dollar fee, much to my own surprise, I adopt a dog. Kind of a backhanded way to do it, just so someone else wouldn't.

I sit for a moment, wondering what my decision will now entail. She's such a big dog for my small house, one that will need an enormous amount of food and, by the looks of that patchy skin, more medical attention than a brief exam. *If it doesn't work out, I can take her back*, I think. *At least I have saved her from the immediate situation.*

So, here she is, sitting in the back of my SUV, a blurry thirty minutes later, head tilted slightly to one side, curious eyes locked on me. My errands will have to wait. I can't leave her sitting in the vehicle in the hot Florida sun. I question my hasty decision as I turn the key in the ignition.

I slide the gearshift into reverse and glance over my shoulder to back out of the parking lot. The dog sits upright. Her head is eye level with mine—her gaze unflinching.

"Don't look at me like that," I tell her. "I'm just as shocked as you are."

4

BEGINNINGS

One week before that fateful day at the shelter, I stumble out of bed and frantically search the living room for my cell phone. The obnoxious ringtone has jogged me to consciousness. A muffled vibration tells me it has fallen somewhere under the couch. Having corralled it with an errant shoe, I sink into the cushions and manage to connect on what is most likely the final ring. It's Charlie. I am suddenly wide awake, relieved to have located it in time.

He is officially a civilian and taking his first steps toward a new normal. I have yet to see him in person, but I am grateful for his safe return. Seconds into the phone call, I sense something is wrong. He sounds breathless, oddly strained. I speak buoyantly, projecting my usually quiet voice in an effort to override my concern. To lighten the tone of the conversation is to instinctively protect myself. While I encourage him to talk, I am fearful of what I might hear.

His duty station had been Kaneohe Bay Marine Base, Hawaii. After an honorable discharge, the military flew him to Colorado. Charlie wasn't from Colorado. He had never actually *lived* there. It was the address he gave when he enlisted and, upon his discharge, it was where he would stay with a cousin. A month later, the government would ship his vehicle to St. Louis, the nearest port. Had I been aware, I would have offered a rental car. He secured a ride, traveling over three states to retrieve it.

Reunited with his beloved Jeep, he is en-route to Texas, just beginning the eight-hundred-mile drive to Austin. Two of his fellow Marines have taken up residence there. Not certain where he wanted to go, Charlie decided to join them. I have never met them—these two young men who have spent the past four years with my son. All three enlisted at the same time. In the same unit, they weathered the trials of boot camp and three deployments together. I imagine their alliance as strong—woven together by shared experience. It makes sense that they will continue the connection.

This is a rare call from Charlie. I sit up to take it in. He had stopped for gas, he says, his voice raspy, tight. The cashier couldn't make change, something about the register. The clerk was foreign, the transaction agonizingly slow. It felt deliberate, insulting, he tells me. His blood boiled as he waited, slowly losing his patience, mumbling obscenities, slamming the counter with his fist. He thought he would explode.

"I almost came across the counter and choked him," he says. "I almost lost it. I... I could've killed him."

"Well, you didn't," I state emphatically. "You got in your Jeep and left. That was self-control."

"Only because people were watching. Damn customers

and security cameras—" Tension laces his voice. He doesn't trust himself, doesn't know if he can restrain himself when anger wells up inside of him, and yet he knows it would be wrong to act on it. He struggles within to control his rage, trying to readjust to civilized society, when where he has been was anything but civil.

I say something about making good choices and the value of not going to jail, before awkwardly changing the subject. "Hope you have good weather for your drive," I tell him. "It's scorching here." I talk about Texas, about his route, about new adventures, anything that doesn't involve killing the poor station attendant. He drives. He listens. He talks a little. His thoughts redirected, gradually Charlie's voice calms.

My mind flashes back to when he was in Iraq on watch patrol. Sitting in a Humvee alone for hours, he found a satellite phone in the vehicle. He called me. It was two in the morning in Florida. I had scrambled to find the right words in my groggy alarm. I may have asked where he was or if anyone could be listening. If I did, he brushed it aside. I talked about nothing and everything. We lost the connection three times. He called back, both of us shocked that contact could be made at all from almost halfway across the world. The sound of my voice seemed to bolster him. The last time the line went dead, he sounded stronger.

Now, on this morning, with the call ended, I sit for a long time clinging to the phone, playing back the conversation in my head, wondering if I had said the right things.

Over the past four years, our rare conversations have elicited mixed emotions. Though always a relief to hear him, I struggled to read the tone of his voice, analyze the delivery, search for hesitations, sighs, cracks in the façade. It's a fine line that parents and spouses of the military walk—the reassurance of hearing his voice—and the anxiety of trying to assess how he was really doing.

I am his mother, I would tell myself. Despite our difficult past, I should instinctively know how he is. To my dismay, I could tell no more than I could from a stranger. Then, there were long periods when I heard nothing and could only rely on faith that all was well. Now, he is out. This phone call, though clouded, is a relief. Four long years are finally over.

But war follows soldiers home. They carry it in their bodies and minds long after their experiences are gone. There is much healing to be done.

5

GROWING UP

CONTRADICTORY TO MY QUIET EXTERIOR, my mind is a silent explosion of random thoughts and disorganization, tiny firecrackers popping off at strange and unpredictable times— all the better to distance myself.

"I don't connect with people," I once offered to a therapist, one of many I have seen throughout my life. "I have an attachment disorder." Ever the defeatist, I braced myself, expecting the words *intervention* or *institution* in her response.

"Being introverted is not necessarily a clinical diagnosis," she replied over the top of her eyeglasses. "It's more a personality trait."

She was right, of course. To imply that I am averse to human interaction may be going too far. My life has not afforded my preference for a hermetic existence, and I *am* capable of functioning in society. But I will be the first to admit that I relish my solitary moments. Retreating is always my first line of defense. And with the exception of my children, I prefer the companionship of canines.

Despite my antisocial nature, I have a history of romantic relationships—though they are a sad trail of ill-fated liaisons. Not long after high school, one such attempt led to marriage, a quick ceremony at a local courthouse—an impulsive move that would shock my mother. Just as abruptly, I filed for divorce. Some years later I tried again, marrying briefly and again quickly divorcing, this time taking two-year-old Charlie with me. That I had married at all astounded me, given my reserved nature. That the second marriage produced a child, thus making *me* a mother, was equal parts shocking, scary, and absolutely amazing.

Enter Charlie—impulsive, headstrong, in constant motion, and diagnosed with attention deficit disorder. I recognized the similarities in my own childhood and silently paid homage to my parents for surviving the trials of raising me. True to my nature, I would raise him alone, which, for reasons of his own, was more than agreeable to my former spouse.

We would struggle, Charlie and I, on a daily basis. It was a poor combination—a child who required extraordinary patience and consistency, a mother who possessed neither. I have a tendency to be hard on things. Mostly this applies to shoes, vehicles, and nail polish, but I was hard on Charlie too. A wiser woman would have been more forgiving, more understanding, and so much more affectionate. A wiser woman would have recognized defiance as a plea for attention.

Those years of raising Charlie were riddled with other

challenges. I received a breast cancer diagnosis, survived a life-threatening blood infection, endured a serious heart ailment and, in a strange turn of events, underwent unnecessary brain surgery. My life ricocheted between raising Charlie and a seemingly never-ending battery of tests, treatments, doctors, and hospitals.

On the surface, I appeared to be a healthy adult. To look at me, one wouldn't have noticed anything amiss—blonde hair, brown eyes, five foot five. I had a strong physique. I was active. I didn't drink or smoke. I maintained a healthy diet. I harbored no preexisting conditions, held no family history of medical perils that I knew of, and yet, in the span of six years, I experienced ailments, one after another, that could easily have led to catastrophic outcomes.

Cancer is scary. Heart problems are scary. Brain surgery... I could barely function at the thought. I had tolerated chemo well, returning to work between treatments. I felt surprisingly good except for headaches that fluctuated in severity, causing the doctors some concern. An MRI was ordered, revealing a tiny shadow near the base of my skull for which there was no immediate explanation.

Suddenly, I was scheduled for surgery. Fending it off, I sought a second opinion. It was *brain* surgery, after all. I pictured no longer being right-handed or suddenly becoming fluent in French. I had dreams of eggs cracking. Images of chainsaws clouded my mind.

I met with top doctors at top hospitals. Exploratory surgery remained the consensus. The procedure itself, a tiny microsurgery, would be intricately precise and much less invasive than I had imagined.

The outcome? Nothing. The official diagnosis delivered directly from the surgeon. It was nothing—a tiny molecular dot that, upon slight manipulation, disintegrated—the true identity never to be established.

Simple and quick, and yet it was still brain surgery. To say that it was nothing was the best news ever. To brush it off as nothing was impossible. In the span of two weeks, I had lived the entire worst-case scenario—put my affairs in order, planned for my child's future, experienced the grave concern on the faces of the medical team, strained to hear their hushed voices during preparation, and waited, in agony, for the results.

And then suddenly it was Monday, and I was ushering Charlie off to school, returning to work, back to business as usual.

It was nothing... and it was everything.

Our chaotic life continued to endure crisis after crisis. My mom, ever the silent supporter, occasionally swooped in and tried her best to help. A church-going, God-fearing force of nature, she had raised five children alongside an emotionally distant husband. In my youth, I had vacillated between a need for attention and a detachment from the chaos. My relationship with her always managed to survive. By this time, she was divorced and living in Florida. It is entirely possible that she simply liked the weather. Having endured our childhood and teen years, I suspect she preferred a physical distance from the challenges her children presented as adults.

On my own, two divorces behind me, functioning poorly as a single parent, and struggling with numerous health issues, I had another child. Of course, I did. I had continued to pursue relationships (if you could call them that) and though I prided myself on making an effort, my choices were less than stellar. I suffered through a string of unsuitable mates, enduring things I shouldn't, tolerating things I needn't, and hoping for things I knew would never be. Inexplicably, I kept trying. I wasn't picky—if he was male and showed any interest, he was the one for me—the drunk at the local bar, the mechanic working on my vehicle, the guy with the charming smile and the long criminal record. It got worse— the seemed-to-be nice guy turned stalker, the husband of my soon-to-be ex-best friend. Driven by my heretofore mentioned need for attention, coupled with a sort of emotional apathy, my standards were low; my morals even lower.

Fallout was inevitable as my poor choices affected those around me. Charlie suffered from my inattentiveness. Friends and family disconnected, one after another. My path to self-destruction might have continued if pregnancy hadn't stopped me in my tracks.

A second child was welcome news, at least for me. Charlie was ten and quite dismayed at the prospect of a sibling. My mother offered no opinion, having long ago turned a blind eye to that which she could not make sense of.

Their sentiments, loud or silent, weren't necessary. I was aware of my limitations. I struggled with depression, harbored major insecurities; my health was a roller coaster, my judgment questionable. Seemingly incapable of maintaining adult relationships, it would correlate that I had no business raising children. And yet, there I was, with one rebellious middle-schooler and a baby on the way. Just as my confidence level was at an all-time low, I had been given a gift of hope. I made a promise to myself that I would live up to the job.

I had nine months to reflect. If I had learned anything from my mistakes, it was not to repeat them. There would be no more relationships for me. This wasn't a stretch. I hadn't had much luck there anyway. My growing belly was a daily reminder to stay away from trouble and didn't allow for the kind of social interactions I had been pursuing anyway. From here on, I would focus on my health, my work, and my kids. My children would get me and only me. Whether this was a blessing or a curse for them, I wasn't quite sure.

Two short years after Sarah's arrival, I was hospitalized again. Leaving work one evening, gathering the kids from homecare and school, I was weak and having enormous trouble walking, so much so that I sat in the car at a filling station and instructed twelve-year-old Charlie on how to work the gas pump. Later that evening, I enlisted a neighbor to babysit while I drove to the ER. Unable to get out of the car, I could only blast the horn from the parking lot.

The diagnosis: bacterial endocarditis, an infection that had entered my bloodstream and traveled to my heart. Coworkers helped. My mom flew in. To my surprise, my dad visited every day. The medical team suggested that the cause might have been an innocuous cut on my arm.

What?

I had lost twenty pounds. Until I could regain my strength, I was in a wheelchair. I had spent almost a month in the hospital fighting a life-threatening condition that had possibly been caused by a small, *very small*, cut on my arm. Upon returning home, it took great effort not to bubble wrap my children for safety purposes.

In the years to come, Charlie would present more challenges. I would add poor judgment, inconsistency, and even more medical emergencies. We struggled through school, suspensions, relocations, hospital stays, old wounds, lousy parenting, and teenage rebellion. In the end, it was a car that was our undoing, or more accurately, the lack of one. It became the one challenge that would not be overcome.

6

THE CAR

In his teens, I transferred Charlie to a different high school, out of his element and away from his friends. My challenging little boy was, by this time, a defiant teenager—railing against school, social norms and, of course, me. Transferring him was a last-ditch effort to ensure graduation. The new school was far from our home and not on our bus route. I drove him to and from school each day. His relentless arguments on why he should have his own car filled the air of the vehicle each morning and again each night—his little sister, belted into the back seat, wide-eyed that her brother might actually *die* if I didn't assent.

Finally, we did it. The car remained a stalemate, but his grades were passing, graduation was assured. When he refused to attend his own ceremony, my mother offered to walk in his place for the photo op. Perhaps we were losing sight of the goal.

"Congratulations," I told him.

"I hate you," he responded.

After graduation, we vacationed in Florida visiting my mom in the gloriously warm weather. The traffic unnerved me, but Charlie helped with the driving. Florida was lovely, a welcome escape from our everyday challenges. Sarah loved the beach. My mom enjoyed the company. Enamored with shimmering sunrises and soft breezes, I considered moving, convinced that Maryland was the cause of my health problems. Charlie met the suggestion with immediate resistance—adamant that he was not moving to Florida.

"It's for old people," he argued. "It's hot."

Ignoring his protests, I landed a job interview during the trip only to suffer a pulmonary embolism on my way to the interview. Crushing chest pains forced a detour to a hospital. A possible side effect of anti-cancer medication, perhaps exacerbated by travel, they explained. I canceled the interview from the ER and remained hospitalized for the rest of our vacation.

Weeks later, back home in Maryland, I assessed the situation. Charlie was eighteen with a diploma. I was alive and well. Filing both under miracles, I researched colleges. He had once expressed a brief interest in video production. It was all I had. I ran with it.

An arts college in downtown Philadelphia looked promising. I broached the subject on a good day. He agreed to give it a try. Success! But it was short lived.

"I'll need a car," he insisted.

"You can walk everywhere," I stated, but his scowl said it all.

Charlie vanished within weeks of moving into his dorm. Days passed with no contact. Sleep deprivation and worry gave way to panic. I had filed a missing person report when he resurfaced in Colorado, the home of my much older nephew who had long ago set out on his own.

"What are you doing?" I questioned him fiercely when we finally made contact.

"Not much. Can't do much without a car."

"A car is the least of your worries," I shot back, frustration exploding from my lips. I am usually a quiet person and, to my credit, my voice *was* rather low, but my hurtful words flowed freely. There was no response on the other end. This failed to deter me. My words spit like daggers through the phone. When I finished, the silence would echo in my head forever.

Days later, with no money, no college, no job, and *no car*, Charlie enlisted. His cousin delivered the news. Then he placed the phone to Charlie's ear.

"If I die, it will be your fault," he told me.

"You'll be fine," I replied, hoping he couldn't hear the terror in my voice.

Over the next four years, Charlie would endure three long deployments to Iraq and Afghanistan, a serious bout with pneumonia, and a life-threatening training injury. In an extraordinary leap of faith now motivated by panic, I would move to Florida with Sarah.

Somehow miraculously, in the midst of the tornado that was our lives, Charlie and I maintained our disjointed connection, the distance and the uncertainty of what lay ahead suddenly bigger than both of us.

Today, four years later, Charlie is in Texas. I am carefully sequestered in Florida. His phone call on this morning reassures me that we can still connect when needed. As he drives to Austin, the conversation helps him check his emotions and regain his footing.

His breathing steady, his tone calmer, we end the call far better than it had begun. Anchored now, he promises to contact me when he arrives. I know it will be a long time before I hear from him again.

7
___

PANIC

WE ALL EXPERIENCE a certain amount of anxiety. It's a fact of life and creates some measure of motivation and precaution. I tend to be uneasy more often than not. An underlying apprehension always accompanies me—a silent demon lurking in the shadows just beneath the surface of my skin, waiting, watching for the slightest innuendo—the mere suggestion that something might be *off*. At its worst, it builds quietly but steadily, distracting me, invading my thoughts, permeating the atmosphere around me, slowly taking control of my body. Soon there is sweating, a tightening of the chest, and a dryness of the mouth. My speech may become halted, my surroundings blur, my heart beats wildly, my mind races, and I feel a little faint. Eventually, it leads to an overwhelming fear that I may be on the edge of something, though I'm never quite sure what.

I had struggled with excessive worry for many years, but Charlie's enlistment triggered a new dimension of distress. My anxiety may have been rooted in concern for his personal safety, but somewhere in the recesses of my mind, my fears became intertwined with my own well-being. My focus turned to my health. I obsessed over a wide array of ailments, lumps, bumps—anything really until I was certain that something was so glaringly, physically wrong that I wouldn't survive the night. This was not without justification. I had proof that bad things happened to me regularly and with no warning.

I harbored other irrational fears: snakes, heights, elevators, public speaking, peeing—and I went to extraordinary lengths to avoid such objects and situations (with the exception of peeing), but this was a more difficult fear to evade. My anxieties were now motivated from behind the scenes, incited by the perilous position of my son, his circumstance so powerful and frightening that I could not wrap my mind around it. So, I didn't. Redirection of the mind is one of our most amazing survival skills—the ability to imagine beyond an overwhelming situation. Typically, I try to redirect to more pleasant thoughts, but in this instance, in some unconscious need to block out the worry over my son, I replaced one giant negative with another.

Adding to my anxious nature is my strong belief that we are watched over by a higher power and, as such, may be rewarded as well as admonished for our decisions in life. Call it karma, call it whatever you like, as I slowly inched my way toward a more responsible adulthood, I deeply regretted past indiscretions and carried with me a foreboding feeling of an aftermath yet to come.

My irrationality seemed to have started shortly after my move to Florida. Sarah, who was eight at the time, shouted directions while alternately singing to a Chipmunks' tape the entire fifteen-hour drive. The trip, the move, the new job, Charlie; the stress was overwhelming. Shortly upon arrival, I remember a funny feeling in my leg.

"A fullness," I relate to my new doctor, an insanely pleasant guy whose demeanor strikes me as a little off. Surely doctors aren't supposed to be *this* happy. *A little more concern would be appreciated.*

"It's too tight," I tell him, sitting on the edge of the exam table, stretching my leg to prove my point.

"Something is *very* wrong," I insist, dropping my voice an octave in an effort to erase his smile. *This is serious, dammit.*

He orders an ultrasound. All is well.

"Are you sure?" I frantically question the nurse who delivers the results. "Pulmonary embolisms begin most commonly as blood clots in the lower extremities. The condition can be brought on by extended travel."

"So I hear," she responds dryly, her irritation apparent through the phone.

Over the next few months, I complain of chest pains, necessitating an EKG, then stomach issues, followed by a colonoscopy. The list continues. For someone overly worried about her health, one would think I would worry about excessive amounts of radiation from X-rays or the dyes that accompany scans and injections. Irrational is irrational, my friend.

"Your tests are fine," the doctor assures me. "Perhaps there is something more going on?"

Indignant at the suggestion that the "more" may be in my head, I find a new doctor.

8

NO GUARANTEE

DID I mention that I'm scared of peeing? Well, not peeing, per se, but peeing too much. That exploratory brain surgery, blessedly unproductive in terms of outcomes, created a slight imbalance in my pituitary gland. The medical term is central diabetes insipidus. Though unrelated to diabetes, some of the symptoms are the same: uncontrollable thirst and the urgency to urinate frequently (more like water than pee and in *extremely* large amounts). Uncontrolled, the condition can cause dehydration, even death. My pituitary gland was no longer able to regulate properly. A synthetic hormone known as vasopressin, applied intranasally at strategic intervals throughout the day, renders the condition somewhat manageable but there is no known cure.

Until I was more skilled at administering to symptoms, I knew the exact location of every ladies' room in every establishment I passed. I would hurriedly excuse myself from meetings, phone calls, and waiting lines. I considered the purchase of a small RV for the sole purpose of having a bathroom available at all times.

Though at first angry and self-pitying, I managed to find perspective. I resigned myself to this new way of life, grateful that the surgery had gone well, accepting that there are inherent risks with any invasive procedure.

Then, almost exactly one year to the day, just as suddenly as it had begun, it stopped. In the ladies' room at work, just as I stood ready to inhale my life-sustaining, nothing-short-of-a-miracle, nasal spray, I realized I didn't need it. I didn't feel that all-too-familiar urgency. I thought my last dose hadn't yet worn off. So, I went back to work. And I waited—no symptoms for an hour. I checked my watch. Twenty-four hours. I held my breath. After a week, I put down the vasopressin. Doctors had no explanation. They had no guarantees.

So, okay, maybe I hadn't actually accepted the situation. I made a brave attempt, but acceptance? I wouldn't *really* call it that. The condition had been forced upon me. I had no choice. Now, a miracle dangled in front of me like a balloon darting in the breeze. Instinct wanted to own it, yet if I touched it, there was a chance it would pop.

I lived in this holding pattern for some time, careful not to let my guard down, just in case. No guarantees, remember? To this day, I haven't properly acknowledged, nor have I ever celebrated the cessation of symptoms.

Sometimes I feel the need to urinate more frequently than usual. I pee a lot when I'm nervous, also when I've had too much coffee. On those days I wonder, I question, and I pray. Sometimes, no surprise, I panic.

I fully realize how silly it may sound to panic because you are peeing, but I remain adamant in my concern. Don't tell me to quit worrying. Don't tell me to calm down. Cancer, blood clots, questionable brain scans, life-threatening infections... things *happen*. I know.

Therein lies the overriding psychological issue of my life. I choose to remain skeptical. There are those who become stronger with each trial that life presents, warriors who have looked death in the eye and prevailed as steadier, hard-as-nails survivors, those who will not be swayed by the next challenge.

Not me, sister. It's not in my make-up. Without a guarantee, of which there are none in life, I live in fear of the next scary thing.

9

THE DOG

My initial surprise at having adopted the dog is nothing compared to the shock on twelve-year-old Sarah's face when she sees her. We had talked about getting a dog but this, not surprisingly, was an impulsive decision, a transaction she was not privy to as she was visiting relatives at the time. The absence that particular morning of Sarah's usual commitments—dance, soccer, music lessons—had allowed free time to stop at the shelter.

Sarah is blonde and tall like her brother, with his same dark eyes, but that's where the comparison stops. Her schoolwork is exemplary. Her room a perfectionist's dream. Self-disciplined, conscientious, and supportive of her older sibling, my younger child puts me to shame daily. Sarah doesn't necessarily benefit from a more mature mother—she is just better equipped to handle the one she has.

I aggravate her with my impromptu ideas and wayward inconsistencies. My anxiety issues overwhelm me at times, rendering me incapable of normal everyday function. My irrationalities anger her. Sometimes they embarrass her. Mostly, though, when I am a complete nut, she just acts as though she doesn't know me. Her coping mechanism is to immerse herself in her own activities.

Outgoing and self-assured, Sarah has cultivated her own close-knit group of friends and relatives. Most of our family members reside in Maryland and, even at her young age, she takes advantage of offers to travel with them. Disney World, the Macy's Day Parade, the Changing of the Guard at Buckingham Palace—she frequently accompanies aunts and cousins to places that I decline to go. Quite the savvy traveler, she can navigate a kiosk like an expert, and though she may wear a Tinker Bell neck pillow and tote a Snoopy suitcase down the tarmac, she exudes the confidence of a seasoned adult.

I recognize the value of travel and fully support the wealth of experience that she gains from it. I had traveled as a youth as well, long before anxiety intervened. I worry, of course, even though she is with adults and family. It's what I do. When she travels as an unaccompanied minor to Maryland, I take great pains to secure nonstop flights. She insists that she is capable of changing planes alone.

"Not on my watch."

I place identification tags on all her clothing and stuffed animals, which she removes with a scowl.

Now, she appears overjoyed to see the dog, although a little taken aback by her condition. "She's skinny. Are you feeding her?" she asks. Always the practical one, Sarah will now carefully monitor every nutritional and health aspect of caring for the dog.

Just as I had predicted, our new companion requires medical intervention. Subcutaneous fluid injections quickly rehydrate the poor girl, while antibiotics and anti-inflammatories fight a respiratory infection and double ear infections. Stubborn skin and urinary tract infections are treated repeatedly. Having been admonished by the veterinarian for her lack of body mass (I'm feeding her!), I receive a prescription for high-fiber dog food. Of course, there are follow-up vet appointments at an added cost. But the dollar signs were expected, and as the dog's health improves, the line between compassion and expense blurs.

Our four-legged friend remains, at first, in a corner of my bedroom, watching us through half-closed eyes, occasionally stretching to readjust her position, seemingly in awe of the comfortable rugs and pillows we have scattered for her on the carpeted floor. Did I mention there is a dog in the house? Back there, alternately sleeping soundly and observing us carefully, is a dog that needs care and attention. That she is back there at all, away from our everyday chaos, feels like a happy little secret that I hold close.

In my younger years, I had worn a locket around my neck, tucked under my clothing. No one knew it was there but me—it's personal and sentimental value more important than any fashion statement. It made me happy just knowing it was there. The sleepy dog in my bedroom does the same, and that empty longing deep in my gut, the one that only a dog can fill is, at last, silent.

Soon, curiosity sets in, and she explores the house, cautiously extending her perimeters to the outdoors. She isn't inclined to wander too far without checking in, just as she had done at the shelter. Indoors, she stays close, so close that it is hard not to trip over her. It seems she has some ingrained need to be physically touching humans in some way.

"It's the Doberman in her," I tell Sarah.

"It's the *crazy* in you." She whispers to the dog.

When I sit on the sofa, the dog sits at my feet, resting her head on my knee. When I am at the kitchen sink, she lays beside me on the newly tiled floor, one paw extended and resting on my foot. Should I shift my foot, she watches patiently until it resettles then places her paw gently on top of it again.

If I am hoping she will ease my anxiety, I am mistaken. Having a dog is important to me, but this dog is anything but calming. The more comfortable she becomes with us, the more irritating she is. Her insistence on being close, body-to-body, face-to-face, breath-to-breath, is an endearing quality, but she is a large dog in a small house, and she is everywhere.

We work with her—really we do—Sarah so much more patiently than I. The dog delights in the training, or more accurately, the attention—but she relentlessly pursues physical contact. She stalks us, waiting for a moment when we are still, then attaches like Velcro as we attempt to move her out of our space, some invisible magnetic force rendering it nearly impossible to push her away. I am not an overly affectionate person. It amuses Sarah as I perch on the high back of the sofa or sprint across a room to deflect the closeness. When the dog sleeps, we tiptoe around the house, giggling at the insanity of it, careful not to wake her and thus enjoy fleeting moments of peace.

She is persistent and restless, still very much a puppy, certainly not the calming influence I had hoped to acquire. Only a few weeks in, I question if she is the *right* dog for me. Then again, even service dogs aren't necessarily born into their calling. It takes years of training and maturity to hone their craft.

Whether she is the *right* dog or not, there is no taking her back to the shelter where her condition was poor and her future unknown. I'm reluctant to give up on animals simply because they don't fit. My last canine companion—a bossy bulldog adopted in her later years and in poor health—ruled my house far longer than anticipated. Every day spent wrestling her difficult attitude was a blessing.

The dog before me now has improved in health, and the time invested in her recovery has been time spent bonding with her. Nia will stay, with all of her exasperating traits. Though Sarah refers to her as "Elmer," referencing the dog's tendency to glue herself to us, it is the name Nia that sticks. A Swahili name meaning "purpose," it seems to fit the circumstances of her adoption. There has to be a reason why this particular dog, unlike anything I initially had in mind and thrown at me in a split-second decision, is suddenly here with us. I had considered the name Mia, for no reason other than I liked it, but it held no meaning in terms of how I felt about her. Other names fell away quickly. Perhaps it was hopeful optimism, but the more definitive name, Nia, seemed to carry a "wait and see" attitude.

I no longer fret about her size. We will simply learn to accommodate. And the haste of her adoption? I have made heftier decisions in less time. There is a dog in the house—a curious, clumsy dog in the house.

Be careful what you wish for.

10

THERAPY

My surgeries made me lumpy. Blonde hair that was lost to chemo has long since returned. Weight once lost to worry, has inched back. All good and normal, yet, with time and healing, parts of me have settled not quite as they previously appeared. Scar tissue has misshapen my body in places. Everything, now, is a lump to me.

I had insisted on mastectomies for both breasts, though only one was affected. I refused to spend my life worrying about the other. My own muscle and tissue were used for reconstruction. My left breast is a stomach muscle. The right is muscle from my back. Pushed underneath my skin in separate surgical procedures, each has survived the trip to its new resting place where it remains viable, the successful product of surgeons. I sport a 14-inch scar across my back that reaches around my body to just under my arm; another scar crosses my stomach. My body is a walking testament to the miracles of medicine. I'm grateful, and yet parts of me are numb where nerves were cut, other parts are lumpy with the passage of time. In the shower, in the mirror, I check constantly for anything unusual. I am terrified of lumps.

I have been to the emergency room nine times in the past year alone. This does not include doctor visits and urgent care clinics. Sarah is in school during many of these visits and not fully aware of the frequency. Somehow I remain employed. My absences, excessive even by my standards, go unnoticed for the most part. I'm largely out-of-sight anyway as most of my time is spent upstairs in courtrooms and not in the office. Coworkers sympathize with my vague excuses, locked in their own battles of stress-related manifestations. Bosses rarely raise an eyebrow as long as I arrange coverage.

I willingly set aside my dignity on my way to the hospital, convinced that this may be my last moment on earth. A lump in my throat is quite obviously a cancerous growth, I will insist, as though the doctors have not been trained properly to recognize these things. It needs to be removed and now. I am willing to bypass any surgical preparation. No need to admit. The emergency room will do just fine. Please take care of it now. I need to get back to work and family. I need to stop worrying.

"Yes," the nurses reply coldly. "That's exactly what you need to do."

I imagine the doctors in the ER nod knowingly each time I arrive. I am certain that my name lights up in red warning signs in some back room when my foot crosses the threshold.

To drive oneself to the hospital, while in the midst of a medical emergency, screams of a non-serious malady. Those arriving by ambulance get preferential treatment—escorted in on stretchers by medical personnel, their symptoms assessed right away, physicians pre-acquainted with the details via radio transmission even before the patient arrives, while the rest of us sit in the waiting room in silent panic.

For a brief, *very brief,* moment, I consider driving myself to the hospital in my own personal ambulance, shooting a heads-up of my symptoms over the radio as I negotiate traffic with sirens blaring. Ambulances are available for purchase through the Internet. Who knew?

I present the idea to my new therapist, a burly, bearded man who holds a pipe between his lips but never lights it. I am merely trying to convey the desperation inside my head when I am in crisis mode.

"Do your research first. They're expensive."

"Excuse me?" It is entirely possible I may have heard him incorrectly.

"It's a bit like driving a U-Haul van, which you can rent if you want the experience first." His eyes brighten, even as he mumbles his response.

I consider his remark and decide he is therapeutically turning the tables on me, though it's not necessary. Clearly, an ambulance is not the issue here.

"I will." I play along, dismayed at his approach.

"Parking could be a problem," he continues in all earnestness. "Diesel can be costly..."

This much I know about therapists, they are hit or miss, some better than others. I've seen quite a few. My visits are sporadic due to the expense, but I concede that they are a necessity in my life. A living person to bounce my insecurities off of is paramount to my sanity, whether they are sympathetic or not.

I leave somewhat perplexed by the conversation. Perhaps *he* is the one in need of medical transport. That familiar panicky feeling churns as I drive home to my little farmhouse, gripping the wheel of my vehicle that, sadly, has no siren.

11

CHRISTMAS 2009

IT WILL BE months before I see Charlie. He moves to Texas and settles in quietly. I stay busy, as always. When we speak, I don't ask much about what he is doing. My previous efforts to manage his life have only resulted in discord. By now, he has clearly survived four years without my assistance. He is an adult. Amazingly, so am I.

"Come for Christmas," I urge in a rare phone call, an effort to connect one Saturday morning. "I'll buy you a ticket."

I had tried his number not really expecting him to answer and, though he sounds unenthused, he agrees. It is done. I will email the flight details and pick him up at the airport. Anxious to see him, I can't wait for the holiday to arrive.

A week before Christmas it rains a light drizzle. Driving to the airport with Sarah, I pretend it is snow hitting the windshield. I abhor northern winter conditions, but it's Christmas. Charlie is coming, and I want a little snow.

At the terminal, we wait in anticipation. Passengers stream by as they exit the plane.

Was that everyone? Had he missed the plane? Changed his mind? Wouldn't he have said something?

The security guard eyes us carefully. The crowd of greeters and passengers disperses, and we are standing alone. I retrieve my cell phone from my purse to call him. Just then a lone passenger appears.

"There he is!" Sarah squeals her delight, breaking the tension in the air.

He had purposely stayed behind he explains, separating himself from the crowd. I quickly relate. Whatever his reasoning, there are far too many people here for me. Carrying a backpack, he seems taller than I remember and older. With rugged features, his face has changed from a round baby face to a more chiseled look. His body appears lean but fit under a long-sleeved T-shirt and jeans. Closely cropped dark blonde hair seems, at first, the only outward indication of a military background. That background includes three deployments, promotions, a slew of ribbons across his uniform and a commendation for exceptional performance, which, when asked about later, he will dismiss as unimpressive. I know better. He had risen to the challenge. He had done well.

With a quick hug and a smile, I try to keep my emotions at bay, knowing it will embarrass him if I cry. It has been so long. The underlying stress that permeated my life during his enlistment wells up anew at the sight of him. He has only been in Texas, not overseas, yet to me, it is as though he has just arrived in the states. That feeling will stay with me for a while. Like a raft with a tiny puncture that slowly releases pressure, almost imperceptibly at first, I begin to exhale. If only all of life's pressures could slowly escape into the atmosphere.

"Do you have a bag?" I inquire.

"No," he responds, "Just my backpack."

Tightly secured against his back, he carries a flat military-issue canvas that, save for possibly a toothbrush, looks empty. As Sarah happily leads him toward the parking lot, I make a mental note that the clothing I bought him for Christmas may be needed earlier.

The next few days are hectic, at least for Sarah and me. We busy ourselves with last-minute preparations for Christmas. As most of our family lives out of state, gifting is not only a matter of shopping and wrapping but also of numerous trips to the post office. We cook favorite recipes and hang more decorations as Charlie sleeps on the sofa. Apologetic that his sleep cycle is "out of whack," he doesn't join in the preparations. He sleeps for days. We work around him. We lay wrapping paper across his body. Having covered the tables and floor with paper and presents, we are in need of extra space. We work on crafts and handmade gifts while seated next to him. Because there is no school, and I have taken time off from work, we eat, watch TV, play card games, and much to Nia's delight, occasionally nap on comforters that we have spread on the floor. I'm relieved to be in the same room with him, breathing the same air, existing in the same space, even if he is asleep.

We stay put in the house this year, which suits me fine. Selfish of me, perhaps, not to share my children for the holiday, not to endure a trip up north, or insist that Charlie meet us in Maryland so that others can welcome him home. To spend Christmas with just the two of them—the two people in the whole world that I feel a profound connection to—is all that I want. And, of course, there is the dog. The dog makes things complete.

Though busy and content, I notice Charlie's prolonged sleeping. If not for brief periods when he showers or sits up to take a meal, I would have checked his pulse to be sure he is still with us.

I attempt to keep him engaged. "How are your roommates?" I inquire. "How do you like Austin?" He will only mumble a few words from beneath the pillow.

Over the coming years, post-traumatic stress, depression, anger, all common challenges of our returning military, will reveal themselves through phone calls and visits that I make to Texas. In the future, I will learn, I will research, I will try desperately to understand, but this Christmas, it begins as a nagging concern creeping around the corners of the holiday— a small voice in my head telling me that something is not quite right.

12

MEETING

Nia has gone insane with curiosity. There's a new person in the house. In typical Nia fashion, she stays close, touching him, breathing on him as he lay motionless, nudging her nose under his arm and pushing with her head until she pops through to the other side, his arm resting across her neck and back. When she thinks no one sees, she climbs up next to him—her efforts thwarted when he pushes her back to the floor.

"Leave him alone," I warn, and she slinks out of the room or drops to the floor, sighing in a dejected heap.

At times, Charlie becomes irritated with her constant touching and mumbles a sleepy, "Go away."

As Sarah and I head out the door, we call to her, enticing her to go for a ride. When she doesn't budge, I announce, "Okay, then... We're leaving the dog here with you."

"Arrrggh," Charlie protests from underneath the pillow that covers his head.

When we return, the two of them lay snuggled on the

couch, both snoring loudly, people arms and dog legs intertwined.

If not for Nia, Charlie likely would never have ventured off the couch that Christmas, so deep is his desire for sleep. Nia will not have it. She maintains a constant vigil over him, breathing her warm breath on his face, alternately whining and sighing while on guard for the slightest flicker of an eyelash or some involuntary movement that suggests he may be waking. Upon detection of said movement, her vigil intensifies. Try as she might to remain still, her wagging tail initiates a shaking effect that starts in her hindquarters and continues through the rest of her body, inch by inch, until she can no longer contain herself. She backs away slightly, spins in small, desperate circles and quickly resumes her bedside surveillance. I am grateful that she is watching. Hovering is so much more acceptable for a dog. Had she not taken the lead, I may have been just as irritating.

Eventually, she succeeds in annoying him enough that he rises to put her outside. Occasionally, he stays out there with her for a while before returning to the couch and to the escape that is sleep.

"She's a good dog," he mutters on Christmas morning, caught up on enough sleep to enjoy a modest celebration. It surprises me that he has formed an opinion about the dog, considering the limited time he has spent with her.

His subdued demeanor is nothing like the wild child that I struggled for so many years to tame. The military has changed him. It has changed me. I marvel that we are together at Christmas, having held tight to the thin line of communication between us, a line that has almost severed so many times over the years, and yet we have not lost contact. I do not wish to credit his military experience as the means to our truce. God forbid anyone should be inclined to send their child off to war as a form of reconnection, but the two of us seem a little stronger now as a result. We have both grown up. Having looked the possibility of dire outcomes directly in the eye, having braved each day of his military service, we have found common ground.

Can we preserve it? Can we build from here? Or will one ill-chosen word set us back?

I extend a cup of coffee to Charlie's left hand, simultaneously placing a gift in his right. In a flash, Nia is between us, ready to assist. Each package she spies becomes one more waiting to be ripped apart. Now, she snatches the package out of his hand with her jaws and drops it to the floor. "Hey!" Charlie exclaims. I cup my hands around his, and together, we balance the coffee. Nia tears away at the present with teeth and paws, bits of saliva-soaked wrapping paper covering our feet. "A little obnoxious when she wants something," he reflects. Scolding her, I reach for the package, commanding her to drop it. She ignores me.

Charlie could use an annoying dog like Nia. She would motivate him to open his eyes, sit upright, walk. Perhaps a slight exaggeration, but his constant sleeping concerns me. I sit down in an adjacent chair and sigh. My son is not the same, of that I am sure. He is here in the room with us, but he is so very far away. His eyes, when they are open, seem vacant.

I watch Charlie recover the soaked present from between Nia's teeth, a vintage T-shirt emblazoned with his favorite band; nothing that a little soap and water can't fix. The bigger issue sits before me. The worry that has haunted me through his four years of service may be gone, but a new worry has materialized. The impulsive, defiant boy is now an adult— sitting quietly on my sofa, barely engaged in the world. But this is not the time or place to voice my concern. For now, I can only wait and see and enjoy the quiet Christmas morning, thankful that he chooses to spend it with us, acutely aware that I have no idea when I will see him again.

"If you come for Christmas next year, I'll give her to you as a present." The words tumble from my mouth. I have no time to stop them. Charlie glances up from the shredded paper. I smother a gasp. What did I just say? Do I not need the dog, want the dog? Hadn't I been consumed with getting a dog?

Nia is a persistent animal that cannot leave people alone. Charlie, it appears, needs someone to motivate him. Of course, she would be good for him. My offer, so quick to roll off my tongue, had been logical and yet, as usual, I haven't thought it through. I don't know where Charlie's future will take him. I'm not sure of his immediate plans or living situation. Will he continue to room with his friends? Does he plan to stay in Texas? Anything but stable right now, he is in no position to take on a dog. Though he might appreciate the offer, I feel sure that he will agree it isn't possible.

"I'd like that."

Charlie's voice interrupts my thoughts, and my internal rationalization vanishes into the air. I know that I have just made a promise. I know, too, that this has always been an integral part of our communication problems. Throughout his childhood, my vague comments, off-hand statements, things that meant little to me, had been promises to him. My inability to see it as such, to just dismiss it as *thinking out loud*, had been at the core of many problems. Broken promises, as he saw them, fueled his anger and distrust. Now, all these years later, I am one word away from letting him down again.

Don't do it. Of course, he should take the dog.

As fickle a comment as it had been to me, it is clear to him. I will not backpedal with a maddening succession of "maybes" or "we'll sees." This isn't the same mother-son relationship that we have almost lost so many times. He is different now. So am I! Have I learned nothing? The last five minutes suddenly seem exhausting. I retreat to the kitchen.

This is an opportunity to get it right. Here he is, sitting before me, barely breathing, but he is here. His interest in the dog offers a connection, if ever so slight, between us. A year is a long time. With the promise of the dog, perhaps he will be more inclined to stay in touch.

And with that, my decision is affirmed. I will get another Christmas with Charlie. Charlie will get Nia. There's plenty of time. Maybe he will be in a position, by then, to keep a dog. Maybe she will motivate him to reach that place.

I steel myself for a reaction from thirteen-year-old Sarah, who has been listening to the conversation. She barely flinches. It's Christmas morning, after all. With her beloved brother home, a mountain of presents in front of her, two horses in the barn, and a new flock of baby chickens on the front porch, had I just given away her cell phone she probably would not have resisted.

13

NIA

ALL TOO SOON, Charlie flies back to Texas, and Sarah and I focus our attention on work and school. Nia focuses her attention on us.

That I am amused by the dog's antics is a blessing, given her intrusive nature. Always underfoot, not a day passes that she doesn't knock over or step on some household object. Chairs, pillows, plates, curtains, even the two of us are constantly in the path of her destruction.

She is smart and dexterous, tapping her paw against her empty food bowl, indicating that it needs to be filled. Soon, she can open doors with a swipe of her foot against the knob. Often, she is a frantic ball of energy crashing through the house. At other times, she can be found sleeping in the middle of whatever room we happen to be in. I can no longer count the number of times we have tripped over her as she lay sprawled across the floor, legs stretched out straight as yardsticks and almost as long.

Some of the furnishings begin to exhibit teeth marks.

One cushion on the couch appears to have survived a shark attack or a canine that desperately needs a nail clipping. An endless supply of dog hair christens every corner of the tiny house. This irritates Sarah much more than it does me. "Behold, the miracle of the simple *broom*." She admonishes me, sweeping a pile of hair out of the front door.

Our renovations begin to take on a ragged look. Walls are scuffed. Doors are scratched. In a matter of months, our newly upgraded farmhouse takes on the appearance of a worn, but comfortable, old farmhouse, which I don't consider a bad thing—I simply didn't expect it quite so soon.

The kitchen floor is routinely covered with water splashed from Nia's bowl that no amount of towel, rug, or placemat can control. A trail of dirt accompanies her each time she bursts through the front door. Stuffed animals and toys scatter the house—an obstacle course that changes hourly, objects dragged and dropped as she makes her way through the rooms, pausing briefly to inspect one or chew on another. It's exhausting. While I am repairing one room, I can rest assured that Nia is dismantling another.

The words *small and quiet* will come back to haunt me as I observe this animal that slowly destroys my home. What was I thinking? I concede that my impulsive nature has gotten the best of me again.

A large dog in such a tiny house presents inevitable mishaps, and one early April morning Sarah slips across the wet kitchen floor and hits her chin squarely on the granite counter top. The sound reverberates in my head. As I rush to her aid, Nia bounds behind me, skidding around the corner in such haste that she can't shift gears. Like a baseball player sliding into home plate, she careens across the floor, legs stretching in every direction, knocking me down as she goes. Ecstatic that both of us are on the floor with her, Nia jumps on top of us, alternately licking our faces and smacking us with her tail. Enter heating pads, ice, and Advil. I tend to Sarah's bruised chin and nurse my sore back for days.

Returning from the market one afternoon, I manage to open the front door with groceries in both hands. As I step inside, I feel a rush of energy behind me, not unlike a wild storm brewing, the wind catching me in its path. It is Nia, of course, the brown whoosh of her body nearly knocking me down as she races by.

"No, no, no, no, no..." I wail, grasping a chair for balance, but I am not quick enough to save the groceries. In one fluid motion, my bags unleash across the floor—muffins escape from their plastic container, and a carton of milk splits on impact. In one corner, a new lamp falls from its perch, courtesy of Nia's tail, and scatters millions of tiny glass shards across the room.

When the dust settles, the dog stands in the middle of the mess, her head tilted, observing with a puzzled look the chaos that she has caused. For a split second, stunned silence fills the space between us—then she dives in to enjoy the spoils.

I hurry to extract her wiggling body from the broken glass, wrapping my arms around her back end and dragging her toward the door. A delighted Nia wags her tail, striking me in the face with each step. After slamming the front door behind her, I return to the scene of the crime. Nia springs at the door, her head continuously popping up in the window like some giant, broken, wind-up toy.

"Stop it!" I yell. "You're never coming in this house again!"

An hour later, when I can stand no more of the incessant head popping, I let her in.

After one particularly long day, I fill her bowl with food and place it on the kitchen floor, amongst scattered broken toys and chewed pieces of my new shoes—the ones I had waited a month to purchase. My eyes narrow at the sight of them. I haven't even had a chance to wear them yet. Sarah skips into the room. Mimicking the dog, she taps the food bowl several times with her toe. "Aren't you going to call her for dinner?"

"I can't," I reply with a slight catch in my voice. Sarah looks up at me. She tilts her head to the side and whimpers. Ignoring the obvious imitation of the dog, I continue between gritted teeth. "You can if you want. I'm not speaking to her right now."

14

THE BOYS

SUMMER ARRIVES and with it the sweltering days of the south Florida heat. The horses sweat. We sweat. The twenty-year-old air conditioner chokes and fumes but thankfully it still works; one less major expense. I decline another invitation to travel with family. New York contains too many people for me. *I'm a homebody*, I tell myself as I pack Sarah's belongings. At thirteen and a half, she chatters excitedly about the vacation, and I will not deny her travel opportunities because of my own shortcomings. Adventures await for those who are willing. I prefer my home turf.

In the days that follow, I realize that I haven't heard from Charlie in months. I try to stick to the old adage that no news is good news, but that nagging worry persists. When repeated phone calls to Texas go unanswered, there is only one way to appease my worry. After making arrangements for the horses and the dog, I sit down at my computer and book a flight. Refusing to travel for pleasure is one thing. Worrying about Charlie is another.

You can do this, I repeat to myself as I drive to the airport, sweaty palms gripping the wheel. I nervously navigate the parking garage, stumble over my words at the ticket counter, and squeeze through the stream of travelers heading to the gate.

Sarah would be proud if she knew—or angry that I would make the effort for Charlie while refusing to accompany her. I shake off the guilt, find my seat on the plane, and struggle, with trembling hands, to fasten my seatbelt.

Hours later in a Texas airport, there is no sign of Charlie. I had sent a text to let him know I was coming, providing my flight number and arrival time. There had been no response. Not surprisingly, he isn't there to pick me up. I call his number several more times and wait. Nothing.

It's getting late. I rent a car and enter the address into the GPS. Traffic makes me nervous too. I'm a good driver, and as long as we're moving, I'm okay. Work-to-home, school-to-store, Maryland-to-Florida, straight shots with a clear destination are preferred. I've never had a panic attack while negotiating traffic, but I've always suspected it was only a matter of time.

Today though, I am on the outskirts of town, not a single vehicle in sight. As I drive, I relax a little and open the car window, inhaling the warm Texas air. It feels like Florida with a little breeze, despite the different terrain. Wide open space surrounds me as I drive down the highway. Outside of Austin, Texas offers room to breathe, unlike the compartmentalized urban sprawl surrounding West Palm. Mesquite trees and salt cedars dot the horizon. No palm trees here. It's beautiful in a kind of wild, desolate way. My mind drifts as I watch the rough terrain spread out as far as I can see.

I appreciate Texas. Having visited several times in my youth, I hold it in high regard. The state drips with pride—in its school system, in its children, in our military. Florida is, well, Florida—glorious weather and beautiful beaches. It holds no particularly strong position on anything, striking me as a haphazard mix of people from other places. Texans, born and bred, seem respectful, compassionate people who defend the ideals they hold strong and reflect a humble but proud way of life. Charlie and his military brothers could have chosen to go anywhere. I feel they are in good hands here.

Soon, country narrows into city, and I am searching Charlie's street for the rental house. Initially rented by the father of one of the boys, they had taken over the lease.

The three had been close since basic training. I have never met Charlie's military brothers, though I have photos of them in my home. In the images, they are standing side-by-side in combat uniform, holding their weapons high. Their faces are covered with dirt. I had printed them from my computer, framed them, and placed them next to Charlie's photo in my home. In such a small house, only a select few gain the privilege of wall space. I routinely studied the images of his companions—covered in dust, a backdrop of mountainous terrain. Grant and James. One dark-haired, one sandy-haired. They look about the same age as Charlie. I have barely spoken to them. Once, when I called, one of them answered Charlie's cell phone but quickly put it down to summon Charlie. That I don't know them personally is of little import. They have watched my son under the direst of circumstances, and he, them. Because they are connected to Charlie, they are connected to me. During their enlistment, their well-being became important to me—as if they were my own.

As I search for the house, I say a silent thank you to higher powers, grateful that these three have returned safely. I can only imagine the intensity of their training and the stress of their deployments. Our soldiers are coming back in droves; damaged and changed—each one facing new challenges. They will need time. They will need help. They will need to find their way; but, by the grace of God, they are coming back.

I knock. No answer. But for two vehicles in the driveway, I would swear the house was vacant—it's peeling paint and dangling gutters desperate for attention. I recognize Charlie's Jeep Wrangler from pictures. An exorbitant amount of debris litters the windows and doors of the vehicle. Parked beside it is an equally neglected Mustang with Texas tags.

The house is brick underneath the paint. It is nestled between two similar houses and located in a typical suburban neighborhood. A tiny front yard struggles to contain an enormous pecan tree. Towering branches threaten to take off the entire roof. Thick roots fracture the sidewalk. Because the tree allows no sunlight onto the front area, there is not a blade of grass to be found. A cement walkway leading to the landing bypasses sand and dirt. Old newspapers are strewn haphazardly around two front steps, thirty or forty papers, maybe more, some so faded they could have been there for decades. I call Charlie's cell phone again, and this time a sleepy voice answers.

"Charlie, did you forget I was coming today?"

"Oh, God," he replies. "I'll be right there."

"Too late. I'm outside your door. Let me in."

And he does.

The door creaks like a haunted house when it opens, and it only opens a little due to the newspapers, but I manage to slide myself in. A cold blast from the air conditioning greets me in the dim interior. I am so glad to see him that I don't immediately notice the trash stacked everywhere or the sparse furnishings. It's the middle of the day, beautiful outside even with the heat, yet they are all, apparently, asleep. They are probably recovering from a wild night out although it seems no one has entered or exited this house for some time. I'm not sure how anyone can maneuver past the newspapers.

I detect a slow shuffling as the inhabitants of the house come to life, and Charlie's two roommates stumble out of their rooms. Unkempt and seemingly unaware of what time or even what day it is, they are here finally before me in the flesh. Though desperately in need of haircuts and shaves, they both possess strong outdoorsman features. One is tall with wavy hair, dressed in sweats and a T-shirt, the other is shorter and wearing a faded blue bathrobe. From the driveway to the door to the inhabitants, it occurs to me that the further I go, the more ragged things become.

Each extends a hand and offers a shy smile. They are nice enough though they seem startled and uneasy to have a visitor. An unmistakable "deer-in-the-headlights" reaction radiates from both, an odd turn of events for me. *I* am usually the one uncomfortable in situations like this, but I am fine.

We talk for a while, all three boys standing before me in the living room. With the exception of a bench press along one wall, and a small tent in the middle of the room, the place is devoid of furniture. In a back corner looms a training dummy, a half torso mannequin balancing eerily on a pedestal, pinkish vinyl skin wrapped in a Mideast headdress. It appears to be peering toward the back yard, a security deterrent if ever there was one.

It's glaringly apparent that Charlie has failed to mention my visit. We fumble through preliminary conversation. In an effort to put them at ease, I mention that I have reservations at a nearby hotel. All three avoid eye contact, preferring to study the worn carpet. My questions elicit short, compliant responses. It feels strangely like an interview, though I don't intend it that way.

"You're Grant, yes?" I ask the dark-haired, bathrobe-clad young man standing closest to me. The scruffy stubble on his chin, black as the hair on his head, makes him appear older than the others. Blue eyes connect with mine briefly, before reverting to the floor. "And you're James? I've seen your pictures."

"Yes, ma'am," comes the stereo response.

James speaks softly and hesitantly, shifting his weight from one foot to the other. His brawny appearance belies a cautious mannerism.

Not at all what I had expected—they remind me more of frightened puppies than soldiers. Military training aside, they don't seem as though they could hurt a flea. I had been nervous about meeting them. Now, my own insecurities fade in comparison.

In some ways, I feel as though I already know them. I had enveloped these two in my concern during their active duty—and I'm usually not overly compassionate about anyone other than my own children. Quietly rooting for them from behind the scenes, I had kept abreast of their unit activities. They had been recipients of my care packages though they may not have known. They were included in my prayers. Standing here with them now, I feel a strong connection. Had they been aware, it probably would have frightened them.

My questions seem so formal. "Are you originally from Austin?" I ask.

"No, ma'am," comes the tandem answer.

"Did you know each other before enlisting?"

"No, ma'am," responding in unison again.

I casually note that the place wasn't hard to find, and the location is great, convenient to everything, and they agree.

"Who owns the Mustang?"

Grant indicates that it is his.

"Nice car. The Jeep, I'm not so sure about..."

They smile a little.

Charlie made the purchase from a parking lot on the base in Hawaii, though it wasn't as shady a transaction as it sounds. The stretch of blacktop was a makeshift used car lot for soldiers. This particular Jeep had been through quite a few owners. It was Charlie's first vehicle, the one that he had demanded so many times, and I had refused to produce.

The Wrangler, with its 4-inch lift, 52-inch tires and front bumper winch, unapologetically presented its share of dents and scratches, broken mirrors, and cracked headlights. It was so encrusted with mud and dirt that I could not tell the color.

Having finally acquired his own transportation, Charlie spent countless hours working on it and eventually just as many hours roaring through the mud and mountains near the base on weekends. The vehicle had endured more than its share of off-road adventures. I doubted that it could be legally driven on a suburban street although it had been used for that as well.

"Thank you for having me," I say sincerely, though we are all aware they had nothing to do with my visit.

They could have dismissed my presence, disregarded me, and returned to their respective rooms. If they had insisted that I leave, I probably would have understood. Yet they stand before me, politely tolerating my presence as I attempt to engage them in conversation.

They are not boys, I reflect, gazing at each of them as they fumble for words. Standing in front of me, they appear not only uncomfortable but also worn from their experience and aged beyond their years. It is the same impression I had when Charlie arrived at Christmas. In the military, they had been well-prepared, expertly trained, and always ready. Here they seem weary and strained, carefully choosing their words, hesitant in their mannerisms. Standing, now, in their small living room, they appear to have dropped suddenly from the twisted sky of a storm. Though they have landed safely enough, they seem still in shock and unadjusted to their new surroundings.

I ask for a brief tour, and the boys oblige. With three bedrooms, a working fireplace, and a washer and dryer in a two-car garage—it is a nice place. The wall that separates the kitchen from the living room contains an arched opening, intended as a pass-through and designed to resemble a little window.

Cute.

I imagine that at one time it was an attractive family home. Now it's more like a trash-filled fraternity house.

Soon after my tour, the boys quietly disperse. I wander out to the backyard patio alone, navigating trash bags piled everywhere. My gaze travels to an old shade tree resting its heavy torso against a privacy fence. The roots spread underneath the panels, lifting and holding the fence tight against the branches. Secure for now, the fence will eventually crumble under the pressure. Much like the pecan tree in the front that is slowly removing the shingles from the roof, something will eventually give. For now, the shade from the enormous trees offers a welcome reprieve from the heat. I'm grateful that Grant's dad had offered the house.

Back inside, I suggest we meet for dinner later, my treat. They hesitate, almost alarmed at the prospect, but they solemnly agree, and I drive to a nearby hotel, check into a room, and unpack.

15

REALIZATION

I AM happy to book the hotel room with its sparkling pool and complimentary breakfast. The boys seem unaccustomed to company, and truthfully, there is no place for me to stay at their house unless I want to sleep on the floor. There's no spare bed, not even a chair or table. And the kitchen—better to eat out than navigate the stacks of empty pizza boxes, soda bottles, and the overflowing trash can.

No one materializes at the hotel to go to dinner, just as Charlie had not appeared at the airport to pick me up. It isn't personal. They had seemed so uncertain about the offer that I am not surprised when they fail to appear. I locate a small restaurant on the lobby level, order a meal, and carry it back up to the room. Sitting on the bed, remotely changing television channels, only vaguely aware of the massive screen in front of me, I put the pieces together in my mind—the condition of the house, unanswered calls, excessive sleeping, the boys' poor hygiene. A clearer picture emerges and, with it, my nagging concern grows.

To be sure, they don't seem in immediate danger. No one is sick or starving. No one is hiding from the law, at least not that I know of. There are no obvious signs of drug deals or other criminal activity. The three of them simply refuse to leave the confines of the house. They vegetate. They hibernate. They don't seem aware of day or night or the passage of time. The hours in this house meld together into one long anesthetized existence.

Can it be that they just cannot take the first steps to integrate back into civilian life? To become employed, return to school, marry, whatever they had planned? I have never been to a real wedding—much too *social* for me. Suddenly, I want to go to Charlie's.

How long has it been? I quickly calculate the time since their return. Eleven months. Have they really been inside the house for almost a year? Other than Christmas, is it possible that Charlie has not ventured farther than his kitchen? They are bright, competent young men. Surely they plan to step outside eventually. Surely they recognize that their lifestyle is not a healthy one.

I reason that their immediate needs are being met. Food, sleep, even entertainment in the form of TV, video, and computer games, are available to them without ever leaving the house. They keep each other company and have the means to connect with the outside world. I ponder whether friends or relatives are concerned. They probably tell family members that things are fine, something I had assumed as well.

And what of the military—the entity that had been so intricately involved with every aspect of their lives for the past four years? There is no government-mandated wellness check. Their exit had been more of a simple, "Thank you for your service gentlemen, now deal with the consequences of your experience."

I continue to flip through the channels, but the screen before me could be blank for all I care. Suddenly, I am questioning everything, and everything is wrong. My concern for Charlie encompasses his two friends as well. There are three young men in this house who, it would appear, are not making a successful transition back to civilian life. I try to focus on solutions as I drift off to sleep.

The next day I buy a grill, a Brinkmann Outdoor Living Pro Charcoal and Wood Smoker—perfect for the backyard patio and on sale at a home improvement store. Grilling qualifies as an outdoor activity. With a cooking surface alone of 725 square inches, God knows it is too big to fit in the house. It weighs almost sixty pounds and fits tidily into an 18x16-inch box. This should have been my first clue as to the amount of difficulty involved. The instructions appear to be in Chinese, and the grill requires intricate assembly. This must be someone's idea of a joke.

I drag the box around the side of the house, clear the back porch of trash, and attempt to fit the pieces together. After several attempts, I have only succeeded in making it resemble an odd-looking soapbox derby car.

The boys observe from behind the sliding glass doors. When they can stand no more of my staggering ineptitude, they venture out as far as the covered patio and help identify the parts that are, by now, littering the backyard. I notice that I am the only one who will leave the patio to retrieve them.

Grateful for the help, I talk with them as I drag the pieces back and forth. They try their best to converse with me, but the sounds of children playing, vehicles passing, and an occasional plane flying overhead distract them. All three are so fixated on their surroundings that they seem unable to concentrate.

While they manage a little awkward small talk, no one brings up the military, and I don't ask. Nor do they offer any recent personal experiences in Texas, great state that it is. I assume this is because there aren't any.

James and Grant have families but imply that they are not nearby and that their family members don't keep in touch. More likely, it is the other way around.

"The pizzas..." I inquire. "How do you pay for those?"

"You pay online," James answers matter-of-factly, trying to fit one unidentified piece into another. "When you order."

"How, exactly, do they get in the door?" I ask, referring to the newspapers barricading the front door.

No one answers. The boys exchange glances.

"You have to turn them sideways," Grant offers quietly. "They're still just as good."

I stop my gathering efforts to digest the comment, imagining the delivery man trying to fit a sideways pizza through the opening, cheese sliding to the edge of the box, the boys vying for the best slices.

Regaining my momentum, I move on to other topics and receive a vague response to each question. Soon I fall silent as we concentrate on the task at hand.

And then...

"How's that dog?" Charlie's question pierces the air.

"Nia? She's good. Crazy..."

Grant and James are suddenly all ears. "What dog?" they inquire in unison. I describe Nia, including some of her latest antics. Their eyes brighten. I swear I see smiles. Suddenly curious and amused, the boys ask so many questions I can barely keep up.

I keep my visit short, only a couple of days, so as not to overstay my welcome. Besides, Sarah will be back from her own travels soon. I need to pick her up at the airport, gather the horses from a nearby farm, and return to my job. By the last day, the boys seem a little more comfortable around me.

"So, Christmas..." I say to Charlie.

"I'll come for Christmas. I like that dog."

I smile at the inference that he will come only for the dog. These boys need help, and there is plenty available to them. A trip to the Veterans Administration will be in order, counseling definitely, medications, maybe. Whether they will be open to the idea, I don't yet know. What I do know is how helpful Nia may be to their situation. If a dog sparks an interest in a person who is otherwise uninterested in life, well, that is therapy in itself. And this particular dog...

She may not be the *right* dog for me, but Nia will be perfect for Charlie and the others. She will engage them. Nia will let them know when she is hungry, and it is time to eat. When the sun rises, she will insist that it is time to be outdoors. She will be relentless. Either that or she will spend her days alone in a dark house with three semi-conscious people who won't feed or care for her and won't answer the phone to let me know that she is okay. I push the thought out of my mind. I have to somehow motivate these three to begin living again, and Nia can help me do just that.

Purpose.

"I guess I could drive," Charlie offers. "So I can take the dog back with me if the offer is still good."

"She will be your Christmas present." I smile, though I doubt that he is capable of making such a drive given that he hasn't left the house since last Christmas. His agoraphobia makes it difficult to step out onto the back porch. We will work something out. I will find a way to transport her. "Just don't expect me to wrap her."

Our goodbyes said, I drag my suitcase across the yard and struggle to load it into the rental car, cursing as I lose a shoe and twist an ankle. The boys watch from the living room window, concern on their faces, but they make no attempt to assist. This is not due to an intentional lack of courtesy on their part. They are polite. They are helpful. They are stuck.

16

EMPOWERMENT

Soon I am on a plane back to Florida. Though feigning
sleep to avoid interaction with the stewardess, my eyes are
wide open to the problem in Texas. I have hopes that Nia can
help, but in the meantime, I need a way to motivate these
soldiers to reconnect with the world. I may refer to them as
boys, but I am well aware that these are highly proficient and
accomplished young men. The matter will require sensitivity
to their pride and respect for their intelligence. I can't barge
in and start demanding change. With the exception of
Charlie, with whom that never was a positive strategy, they
barely know me.

Gazing out the window, I watch as cottony soft clouds
drift aimlessly across a baby blue sky. Self-doubt creeps in. I
have problems of my own. I am no expert on the fallout of
war. There are other parents involved here. Perhaps, when it
comes to James and Grant, I should mind my own business.

All solid arguments, but it's too late for that.

Compassion has enveloped me. I feel *necessarily* involved

in the well-being of these boys. My feelings are strong, much to my own surprise. Charlie's roommates have been officially added to the short list of people I consider important in my life, a list that has only included Charlie, Sarah, some scattered family members and, of course, my mother. Now, there are two more. "And the dog," I whisper. "Of course, the dog."

A sudden bump of the plane rouses me from my thoughts. Even in the bluest of blue skies, there can still be turbulence. "I have to take medication for this," the woman beside me says, gripping the armrest of her seat. "I hate planes." I flinch, suddenly registering the rockiness as the seatbelt light flickers on, and the stewardess sinks into a nearby spot. A rush of heat flushes my face and neck. I tear my gaze away from the window.

Dammit. Don't you have enough worries without adding fear of flying? Push it out of your mind. You have to fly. If you succumb to this, how will you be able to help Charlie and the boys in Texas? It's a ridiculously long drive from Florida.

Irritated, I am determined to stay calm. I unbuckle my seatbelt and squeeze past my flustered seatmate, my purse colliding with her ashen face as I move through the tight passage. Accidental, yes, but I make no apology nor do I offer sympathy. I am intent on removing myself from any hint of panic. Power of suggestion be damned—this woman is on her own. *I will not let this happen. I will not allow this to happen.* My mantra is empowering. Motivated by anger, I brush away thoughts of succumbing to another irrational fear.

Standing in the aisle, I assess the situation from my better viewpoint. The plane is nearly empty! It defies explanation that, out of all the rows to choose from, this person has chosen mine. "Sit down," the stewardess hisses from her position toward the back, and I obey.

Several rows away from my original location, I secure myself into a window seat, this time with no company. I take a deep calming breath and acknowledge my success—a psychological pat on the back, even if I did hit the poor woman in the head. My thoughts return to Charlie.

It has been seven months since I last saw him. Why hadn't I visited sooner? So intent on tracking his movements when he was in the service, now I am much too lax. Had I really let the months slip by so easily? As the plane lurches forward, my stomach turns at the realization of how long the boys have been in the Austin house. Charlie's phone call, as he drove from St. Louis to Texas, should have been a red flag that he was having trouble. How was it that I had brushed it aside? *And Christmas?* Every part of my being had warned me that something was wrong, and yet I had done nothing.

Now, there are three. They aren't seeking reassurance. They aren't asking for help. I am not even sure that they are aware of a problem. Not knowing James or Grant well, I'm not in a position to discuss it with them, at least not yet. Maybe all they need is someone to gently point it out to them, maybe just a gentle push back into the world that they seem to be making every effort to avoid.

17

_____

PERSISTENCE

As July slowly simmers into August, I make a deliberate effort to stay in touch and become somewhat aggressive at it. If my call goes unanswered, I call again the next day, twice the day after, three times the day after that. On a quick break at work, at lunchtime, on my ride home, I am relentless until Charlie answers the phone. I call in the middle of the day to wake him and to ask if he has been outside. His voice sounds groggy as he reluctantly endures my battery of questions. "What's the weather like? What did you do today?"

When this fails to motivate him, I try a different strategy. I send FedEx boxes with snack foods, just as I had religiously mailed overseas during his deployments. To retrieve the box, one would have to open the front door, though merely setting foot on the threshold is not the same as going outside.

I begin sending envelopes. There is nothing of particular importance in them—a card, a letter, some photos—but I know that they won't be dropped on the doorstep. To retrieve these will entail not only opening the door but walking across the yard to the mailbox. It's maybe ten feet or so, but it counts as a walk. I am sure they occasionally step out to the mailbox —after all, they have to pay rent and retrieve utility bills—but when I inquire, Charlie sleepily offers that these things are done online.

Of course. I sigh.

I pay my bills online too. The boys aren't incapable of taking care of things. They are only averse to leaving the house.

I step up my efforts to lure them outdoors, sending gift cards to local restaurants, texting ahead so they will expect the envelope. I carefully choose vendors for their *lack* of convenience—no delivery and no emailed coupons. The boys will have to get dressed, drive there, and speak to an employee.

I send firecrackers, boldly lying to the post office clerk that my package contains no explosives, hoping the boys will go outside and not set them off in the house. (Years later, Charlie will correct me. "Not a fan of fireworks." he will say, dismissing a New Year's celebration.)

I mail accessories for the outdoor grill, small landscaping items for the yard, a Frisbee. If they see a pattern forming, they never let on. I follow the packages with more phone calls. "Did you try it?" I ask. "Did you like it?" "How was the restaurant?"

Charlie's responses are vague. He avoids any topic that involves going outside. I imagine that packages are piling up at the front door, and envelopes and gift cards probably fill the mailbox by now.

I work the conversation to keep him engaged and open. The phone is my remote control as I try to motivate him from afar, pushing different buttons, hoping for success. Curiosity will surely win. Someone will eventually step outside, won't they?

18

STRESS

In October, Nia begins sporting the latest in Sarah's daily line of homemade Halloween costumes. On a Friday, bright orange polish glistens on the dog's nails. Saturday, I am following a trail of shredded tissue through the house, remnants of a mummy costume that lasted only five minutes. Sunday, a sheet, a belt and two paper plates transform her into a table, set for two. Monday afternoon, a can of green spray paint is swiftly removed from the front porch seconds before she becomes an alligator. The plan is replaced on Tuesday with a fabric alligator costume, complete with open jaws that slide over her head (this one much less messy and easier to remove). By Wednesday, Nia has taken to hiding under the sofa until she is sure that Sarah has vacated the premises.

Sarah has plans to spend the upcoming weekend at a friend's house to prepare for the holiday. "We're making a haunted house!" she excitedly tells me. "I'm in charge."

"Of course you are."

I am in charge, too, I tell myself as I book another flight to Texas. With Sarah away for a weekend, it's another opportunity to check on the boys. She is welcome to come with me, but she has little interest in being cooped up in the Austin house while the boys sleep.

"Oh, what fun," she responds facetiously.

"It's a little like a haunted house," I suggest, and we both smile at the weak comparison.

Reviewing the route to the airport daily, I pack and repack my carry-on a week and a half ahead of time. I refuse to wait until Christmas to see Charlie, but with the anxiety of travel looming large, I find it hard to stay focused. Sadly, the stress, even in this mild form, inevitably wears me down.

October is also hurricane season in Florida, and we are battered with high-intensity electrical storms and torrential downpours every afternoon. The dampness of the air takes a toll on me, and I develop a cough. A rational person would visit a pharmacy, purchase an expectorant, wait it out. I am not a rational person.

Soon I have lost all common sense. I feel sick, achy, and weak; hot then cold. This is something bad—I am sure of it. Fears of lung disease, emphysema, COPD, and cancer haunt me. I take off work, call my doctor's office and ask to be seen today, this morning, *now*. My backup plan, if they can't fit me in, will be the ER. The closest one is eight minutes away.

In full panic mode, I tick off symptoms in my head as I sit alone in the waiting room at 8:00 a.m. The nurse calls me in, takes my blood pressure, and asks me to step on the scale.

"Ten pounds lighter," she remarks. "There's something wrong."

I gasp. UNEXPLAINED WEIGHT LOSS. It is at the top of my symptoms list.

"Oh, not with you, honey, with the scale," she assures me. "Let's try another one."

Too late. My overwrought imagination is planning for the end. How will I tell the kids? How much time do I have?

I'm sure I must have followed her down the hall to another scale. I'm sure it was accurate. I'm sure that I followed her back to the exam room. I must have conversed with the doctor. I don't remember a thing.

"You have a virus," the doctor tells me. "Go home. Stay in bed for a few days if you can. I'll call in some medication."

I stare at her blankly.

"A virus," she repeats louder, as though I can't hear. "It's going around."

It takes a while, but I am able to wrap my head around it as I drive to the pharmacy, relieved that I can stop planning my funeral for now.

"I have a virus," I tell the pharmacist just to hear myself say it. He backs away slightly, nodding in sympathy.

"Feel better," he says, stretching his arm generously across the counter to hand me the prescription.

"It's just a virus," I repeat and, though my hands are still shaky, I'm smiling with the statement. "It's going around."

19

ACCEPTANCE

SOON, I am feeling stronger and determined not to interrupt my schedule. With flight confirmation in hand and Sarah off to organize her Halloween adventure, I take a deep breath and escape the tropical lunacy. Four hours later, I am in Texas once again.

Same scenario. No one arrives at the airport to pick me up. I know the drill. Heading to baggage claim, I make a mental note of which rental car counter has the shortest line. As I stand to wait for my not-quite-small-enough to qualify as a carry-on suitcase, I feel a presence behind me and turn to see James and Grant completely motionless, only inches away. Shocked to see them, I spontaneously hug them both at once. *Me. Hugging.* They bristle slightly at the connection but stand stoic and endure it. They look disheveled, unkempt —homeless-looking would not be an exaggeration—but here they are, waiting behind me. Sans Charlie, they have driven the old Jeep to pick me up.

How long had they planned to stand there? Would they have spoken if I had recovered my bag and walked away?

That they left the house and drove to the airport impresses me so much it makes up for the trouble they have speaking with me. We drive to the house in silence. The Jeep sputters, spits, and stalls at every traffic light and stop sign. Unable to maintain in idle, the engine shuts down each time the speedometer drops below twenty miles per hour. I sit in the back grinning stupidly from ear-to-ear as we wait at each intersection for it to rumble to life again, elated that they have picked me up, delighted that they accept my presence. I don't even ask where Charlie is, preferring to bask in this small victory.

As we pull into the driveway, they practically run me down in their hurry to get into the house. I smile as Grant dons his familiar bathrobe, and the two instantly retreat to their respective rooms.

After retrieving my suitcase from the Jeep, I check the mailbox. Sure enough, it's brimming with envelopes, all from me, although there are no packages on the doorstep.

"Yeah, we almost couldn't get the door open to go to the airport," Grant explains later that evening. The small boxes have been tumbled into the hallway closet, the door of which is now difficult to close, making entrance into the house even tighter.

As I had suspected, no one has ventured from the house since my last visit. Something akin to a mini-Christmas follows as they open all the packages. Charlie even wakes up to say hello and to join the excitement.

The housing situation shows no signs of change, and

during this visit, I drop not-so-subtle hints about veterans benefits and assistance, depression, and post-traumatic stress, all of which I have researched obsessively. I steer the conversation in that direction whenever I can, albeit in a delicate manner so as not to confront or alienate them. I have come equipped with folders and handouts acquired from my local Veterans Administration. I leave them strategically around the house, hoping to open their eyes to the struggles of other military veterans and the assistance available to them.

I counter this with an upbeat attitude and a desire to learn more about the boys. I ask about their families, their backgrounds, why they had joined the military. With some encouragement, James and Grant slowly begin to talk about themselves. Grant, the more forthcoming of the two, notes that he has a large, extended Texas family. His father and grandfather were veterans. He has a brother who lives close by and who sometimes visits. When his father relocated to northern Texas, he suggested that the boys take over the lease. He tells me the robe had been his grandfather's, although I hadn't dared to ask.

So, Grant has returned to a familiar area. He has favorable connections with family, unlike James. The robe, I am sure, comforts him as well.

James mentions a mother, sister, and younger brother, none of whom live in Texas. He had followed Grant to Austin when their military service ended, and the two stayed in touch with Charlie until he joined them. They both seem mildly surprised that I take an interest in them, and for a brief period, the house doesn't seem so dark.

Until now, they knew only minor details about Charlie's

background. They have spent years together surviving threatening situations, protecting each other's lives and yet know very little about one another. Grant and James safely assumed that Charlie had a mother, but he never spoke of one. It surprises them to learn that he has a younger sibling. They cannot recall where he is from, although they feel sure that he may have mentioned it. These details didn't matter in the arena of war. As soldiers, they connected, regardless of background, family situation, or the reasons that brought them there. Despite knowing little about each other's pasts, they regard one another as brothers.

They ply me for misadventures of Charlie's youth and I oblige, occasionally eyeing my son for signs of disapproval. The boys open up about their own upbringings, and we enjoy a laugh at childhood antics. Grant has a sharp wit when he is relaxed enough to joke. He takes great pleasure in ribbing the others about boot camp. He has a way of turning tough situations into comedic exploits, though I am sure the experiences lacked any light-heartedness at the time. That the serious nature of past experience can be temporarily lifted through Grant's anecdotes is a gift, I suspect, which has served him well. Military talk is limited to boot camp. I don't push. Whatever their reasons, talk of deployments is closely guarded.

Two days in, I have established a foothold in the house. The boys no longer act nervous or uncomfortable around me. On the second day, they mostly ignore me, and I am careful not to disturb their mundane existence. Quietly integrating myself into the house, I sleep in Charlie's room rather than stay at a hotel. Charlie retreats to a futon he has moved into the cold, empty living room. First, though, so as not to alarm me, he draws my attention to an enormous collection of guns that he stores underneath his bed. There are more in his closet.

I'm not alarmed. I am terrified, although I don't show it. They have accepted me into the house, and by God, I am staying. I carefully lay crossways at the top of the bed and make a mental note not to shift position in my sleep, lest I should set something off and accidentally shoot myself. Firearms disturb me given the boys' fragile mental state, but I am not here to approve or admonish.

As I lay in bed at night, mice scurry in the walls behind my head. *You've gotten this far. No bailing to a hotel. You're not budging.* I exert as little movement as humanly possible while covering my ears with a pillow.

During the day, I wander the house in sweats and a heavy wool coat that I have extracted from a hall closet. Except for my resemblance to an Antarctic native, I try not to draw attention to myself. I troll the internet in Charlie's room, wash laundry in the garage, do my best to repair little things around the house, clean and clean some more. There is no shortage of cleaning to be done. I meld into the fabric of the house. At times I appear swallowed up by it, but I am there, somewhere behind the stacks of dirty clothes and pizza boxes. Cleverly disguised as a visiting mom, I have infiltrated their world hoping to motivate them out of it.

Not surprisingly, the boys prickle at the mere suggestion of going outside.

"Um, not today," Grant replies as if there is simply no room in his busy schedule.

Offers to see a movie or explore the neighborhood elicit hesitation and a mumbled, "No, thank you."

Charlie is more straightforward in his refusal. "Maybe later," he says. "Maybe next year." Once he simply looks at me and states, "I can't." His expression is so sincere, his voice so kind, I don't, can't, ask for an explanation.

A missed opportunity to talk about it, I know, but I proceed delicately. Charlie and I have never cultivated deep conversation. We spent years yelling at each other. It was what we knew. More recently we are better, we can communicate, but on this sensitive subject, we must learn how to talk.

"Leave their front door open," Sarah suggests when I call to check on her.

She is staying with her friends for a few extra days. They all ride the same bus to school and Sarah, soon-to-be fourteen, enjoys the independence. The arrangement has allowed me additional time with the boys. I feel guilty about extending my visit, but I make sure we talk each evening. She appreciates the extra time with friends and has a genuine concern for Charlie, although on this evening she makes light of his situation.

"Leave a pizza out on the lawn." She laughs. "Or tell them the house is on fire."

Thus follows a list of suggestions designed to entice the boys outside, each one more hysterical than the last.

"Tell them there is a Playboy model at the door."

"Or they've won the lottery, but they only have ten minutes to claim their millions at headquarters!" I suggest.

"Good idea! They'll *run* out the door." She pauses, "Just make sure..."

"Grant isn't in his bathrobe!" we say at exactly the same time.

Our silly scenarios connect us, but I miss her and long to get back.

"I'll be home soon," I tell her.

"Okay. Bring Charlie with you." She sighs.

If only it were that easy.

20

LEARNING

In my initial ignorance of PTSD, I had assumed that each soldier's reaction to war would be individual, but the boys seem strangely similar in their troubles—their desire for sleep, their reluctance to talk about any issues, a slight defensiveness if I push a little too hard, an effort to abstain from outside contact. Are they simply picking up on each other's emotions? Had these three been so connected during active duty that they continue, on some underlying level, to have the exact same reactions?

My research proves otherwise. There is nothing extraordinary going on here. There are thousands of soldiers just like them. Anxiety, discomfort in crowds, isolation, withdrawal from social situations, the same symptoms surface again and again. Those soldiers that do brave the outdoors share mutual aversions as well—a refusal to park near other cars, disdain of loud noises, and anxiety around small children. The soldiers in this house are far from alone in their symptoms.

Through Facebook, they learn of more brothers who have died on active duty. They tell me several soldiers have ended their lives after discharge. Should I detect even a hint that Charlie or his friends are on the edge, seriously contemplating a desire to cease existing, I am prepared to take more desperate measures—call in professionals, quit my job, pack up Sarah, leave the horses with someone, anyone, and immediately move to Austin—whatever it takes.

I don't see it at this moment. I don't see any extremely alarming behavior. I observe no erratic mood swings. I sense no despair in their voices. No one seems particularly preoccupied with death. Maybe they are better when I am here, their moods lightened by having a visitor in the house, but I watch carefully for cracks in their demeanor.

If they had ever been in that state of mind, perhaps it was upon their immediate return or during the ten months that I was unaware of their isolated lifestyle. The possibility had crossed my mind during Charlie's Christmas visit, but I brushed it aside. If the thought had existed for any one of them, would they have helped each other? Would they have reached out?

The question churns sickeningly in the pit of my stomach. Then, just as quickly, I dismiss it. No good comes of dwelling on the past. All I really know is that they are here, existing. Not moving forward, but existing, nonetheless.

The grill seems to be a hit, and it involves brief intervals on the back patio. Their chivalry in helping me to prepare a meal, coupled with the mystifying man-barbeque connection, is just enough of a push to force them outside—exactly as I had hoped.

Because I am the only one who will venture away from the house, I supply meats and fish for the grill and stock the refrigerator with juices and milk. I reintroduce them to fresh vegetables and fruits from a local market. Strawberries and peaches glisten on the kitchen counter, a reminder of simple pleasures.

On my last evening, we all sit down to watch a movie. As the four of us sit side-by-side on the futon, I glance over at them. All three boys sit upright, staring straight ahead at the television in silence, as though they are at military attention. Against a far wall, the training dummy lends a silent stare. Wearing a sheet and sporting a cowboy hat, he appears fixated on the screen. Grant, as usual, is wrapped in his robe.

Should a passerby have glanced in the window, our movie night might have passed as a typical yet mildly awkward family moment (with the exception of our rubberized friend in the corner)—the internal struggles in the room imperceptible to others.

Oh well, at least there is no immediate hurry for any of them. In this safe little cocoon of a house, disconnected from the outside world, they have the luxury of time to recover.

Unfortunately, that is about to change.

21

COUNTDOWN

THE NEXT MORNING, I rise early and go for a walk through the quiet Austin suburb. I have a plane to catch in a few hours, and I'm concerned about the possibility of blood clots. I need to stretch my legs before the flight. It's warm out for October, but the air is fresh and clean, and I'm eager to explore the neighborhood.

As I roam, I consider the irony. In Florida, I rarely venture from my daily path—the local market, the corner gas station, the feed store. I'm sure others have a similar routine. Mine is carefully constructed to limit human interaction.

The gas station in town is never busy in the morning. I get up early on Wednesdays and fill up on my way to work. I always pull up to the first pump; not in an effort to be polite, only to ensure that I won't get boxed in and, God forbid, have to ask someone to move.

The feed store, crowded on the weekends, is open late on Thursday evenings. Nobody goes on Thursdays, except me.

The girl at the counter wears earbuds and doesn't acknowledge me. This makes it even better.

One particular cashier at the market acts equally distant. I pick his line on purpose. He shuffles my groceries through quickly, rarely looks up, and never attempts menial conversation. I'm always relieved.

The hair salon in town is predominantly Spanish-speaking. I listen as conversations ebb and flow amongst the stylists, content to be unable to join in.

I couldn't build a higher wall around me if I used a step ladder. Besides my horses, I can't remember the last time I enjoyed an outdoor activity. Even riding is usually done on my own property. *My world is so small.* Sighing, I navigate the tree-lined streets, kicking up a pile of leaves on the pretty Austin morning. To step away from my life in Florida is to have a clear view of the fog that envelops it.

Charlie didn't possess my reclusive tendencies. He was born an adventurer. It isn't a natural inclination that is holding him back. As I walk, I try to imagine that the rustle of leaves at my feet is something sinister, that a passing car is a threat, that a sunrise is unwelcome when it removes a protective cloak of darkness. I can't. I haven't been where they were, haven't experienced what they have seen, smelled, felt, heard. I haven't relied on vigilant hyperawareness to stay alive. I am not suspicious of movement, shadows, or quiet. At one time, the outdoors was one long adventure for Charlie. I hope he will remember.

The sky has become overcast. A fat raindrop splatters against my cheek. Locating a shortcut through an ivy-covered alley, I head back to the house. When I return, I check the mailbox—the rusty old mailbox that never has anything in it that isn't from me. Habit, I suppose, to check it, just like I do at home. I fully expect it will be empty.

The letter is large, official-looking in its postmark. I squeeze through the front door and hand it to Charlie as he shuffles sleepily down the hall.

"It's from the realty company," he says. He sets the envelope aside and walks away. I pick up the letter. Final notice. Non-payment.

A few phone calls later, we all realize the situation. The money that they pay each month for the rent has been squandered by the owner. With the mortgage now impossibly behind, legal proceedings are underway. The house will soon be in foreclosure. The bank will probably sell. The boys will be out of a place to live. *Lovely. Just what they need right now.*

Rain begins to beat steadily on the roof. I search the house for an umbrella to take to the airport.

22

THE ART OF NOT PUSHING

As I TRANSFER my folded clothes from Charlie's bed into my suitcase, I broach the subject of the VA, choosing my words carefully. "You know," I begin, "a lot of soldiers have trouble when they get out. Someone to talk to, a professional, wouldn't be a bad idea."

"What are you trying to say?"

Charlie hunches at his desk, staring at his computer. At my urging, he has been hunting for a new place to live, the screen a silent reality check jumping out at him in the form of rental amounts, lease options, availability. Requirements include current employment, a good credit report, and a substantial deposit, all of which evade him. Until recently, his immediate needs for housing and food have been taken care of by others, first me and then the government. He has never actually been self-supporting.

Ah, the unpreparedness of youth, to be so blissfully unaware of life's realities.

"You think there's something wrong with me?" Charlie interrupts my thoughts.

"I didn't say that," I answer gently but firmly.

I know from experience that he can twist my words, and this is already delicate territory. I have to be concise yet sensitive. He has allowed me into his protected world, but, in trying to help him out of it, I run a risk of alienating myself.

"I'm just saying that that's what the Veterans Administration does, among other things. They are there to help you guys get back on track." I hadn't meant to imply that anything was off track. I try again. "They can help you figure out what you might want to do now, what direction you want to go." That sounds better.

He is silent.

"You can look it up," I offer. After all, he is sitting at his computer. A world of information for veterans lies in front of him.

"No, mom." Charlie sounds firm, his voice suddenly low. "There's nothing wrong. I'm fine." Through his hair, now almost shoulder length, I can see his ears redden with anger. "And I'm not going to the VA."

I let the subject drop. Enough for now. I know what's at stake. I had spent the early years of his life so at odds with him that I almost lost him. His enlistment had brought us closer, along with the realization that I could have easily lost him to war. Now I run the risk, once more, of losing him if I push too hard, and in my worst nightmares, losing him if I don't.

That final thought pressing against my heart forces me to persevere, to push when I can, and to back off when I need to, but most importantly to stand strong. It needs to be said, and no one else in this house is going to say it. I will maintain this delicate balance. I will not be swayed.

Their psychological state is an awkward dilemma for all three of them and one that they have no control over, at least not yet. Formidable, seasoned soldiers, grown men, they have endured backbreaking, burdensome work, grueling training, murderous tasks. They had been cocky smart alecks, challenging authority, and each other. Today they are unable to step outside without overwhelming anxiety.

The polarity of their existence then and now seems almost unfathomable. Their inability to admit it to themselves and to others, by way of seeking outside assistance is complicated, buried somewhere between dignity, pride, and their understanding, recognition, and ultimate acceptance of their circumstance.

And yet, they need to come to terms with their situation, and quickly. There is no realistic alternative. They can't continue to ignore it or hope it will just go away. It exists, and they need to confront it. Something has to give, and soon.

23

CHRISTMAS 2010

I LOOK FORWARD to Christmas hoping that Charlie may appear, though I caution myself not to be disappointed if he doesn't. Austin to West Palm Beach is one thousand, two hundred and eighty-five miles on Google Maps, a major feat for someone who won't leave the house. Granted, the Jeep offers some protection from the world. Navigating around in an enclosure that can be locked, windows up, radio on, is safely isolating, as long as he doesn't need to get out for long. *Kind of like George Jetson*, I muse, *riding around in a spaceship, protected from the atmosphere.* It is possible to get gas while having no human contact. I'm quite experienced at the maneuver myself. He would never have to get out for food if he packed enough to eat. Pizza keeps relatively well and tastes good cold.

Can the promise of the dog really motivate Charlie to make the trip? After all, a dog can be obtained at a local shelter, just as Nia was. He could easily change his mind, although I hope he won't. I know he can do it. But will he?

I decline, again, an invitation to spend time with friends and family up north. *Charlie is coming,* I tell myself—though I prefer the security of home, regardless.

I hear nothing from him. Sarah and I spend our free time putting up Christmas decorations. Nia spends her time taking them down.

Two days before Christmas, my phone rings. It's Charlie. He is an hour or so away. "What's that exit again?" My heart leaps.

"He did it!" I exclaim when the call has ended. Sarah looks up suspiciously from her breakfast at the kitchen table. "He's on his way!" I yell, though she sits less than three feet away.

I dance around the kitchen, under her disapproving eye. At thirteen, she is much less tolerant of my behavior in general, never mind my behavior when panic strikes. Feigning dejection, I return to the dishes in the sink, but my heart bursts with excitement. I happily chalk this one up to Nia as the source of Charlie's motivation. The dog, lying at Sarah's feet, lazily chewing on her sneaker, has, at last, earned her keep.

After a day of recovery from his drive, Charlie seeks out Nia, and the two of them spend time in the yard. They take short walks and play together along the perimeter of the property. As they become reacquainted, I give them their space, marveling that he has driven all that way for the dog. His demeanor seems a little better, although he has no desire to venture farther.

He declines offers to sightsee. No beaches or parks for him. Fair enough. A safe haven. Isn't that what home and family are for? Respecting that he is not quite ready, Sarah and I indulge in a Christmas lights tour without him.

The holiday comes and goes all too soon. It is time for goodbyes. Sarah's concern for Nia prompts an impressive display of organizational skills as she packs Charlie's Jeep to perfection. Ten large bags of dog food are neatly compressed and stacked on one side of the back seat, ensuring that there will be no food shortage for a year. Nia's dog crate is folded between Charlie's own belongings and Christmas gifts. Her bed is rolled up on the other side, next to his sleeping bag. No hotels for these two. Charlie will pull over and sleep in his vehicle when necessary. Knowing Nia, she will sleep on top of him. The pocket of one door holds her leash, a perfectly folded rabies certificate and, of course, her favorite stuffed toys, carefully aligned in order of Nia's preference—this from the girl who feels compelled to straighten cereal boxes on grocery store shelves. Charlie and I roll our eyes as we carry items to the car.

Happily anticipating the car ride, Nia wriggles and squirms in the passenger seat, whining in agony at the wait. Mature now and no longer undernourished, her body fits tightly in the only remaining space available. Charlie has successfully driven to Florida, careful to remain somewhat secure inside his vehicle. But now Nia is going to go with him, the dog that will not be confined. I can only hope he is ready for her.

"Just try to keep her on her side," I warn, noting one brown paw already in his lap. After our goodbyes, Sarah and I stand in the driveway, blinking as the Jeep kicks up a trail of dust down the dirt road. That vacant feeling rises from somewhere deep inside me, and I swallow as a lump forms in my throat.

"You're not gonna cry, are you?" Sarah asks sternly.

"Oh, I might. You never know with me." Instead, I smile at her as we head back to the house.

I cannot yet know the impact that a dog, this dog, will have on the boys. Nia has a big job to do. I'm not exactly sure what her "big job" will be, but anything seems better than nothing. She has created a spark. A flicker of light now glimmers in Charlie's eyes, and she has already motivated him to leave his house to retrieve her. James and Grant are eager to meet her. The dog that has no respect for personal space is about to infiltrate their carefully secluded world. I am going on blind faith that this may be just what they need.

And if it doesn't work? It's a sudden change for her, leaving all that she knows. For all of her lunacy, Nia is a sensitive dog, and she's attached to us. Will she adjust? And will a person who isn't taking care of himself be able to take care of a dog?

It's too late to worry now. Besides, if there is a way that a dog can pick up the phone and let me know how things are going, Nia will find it. I am saying goodbye to Charlie again, but this time I am saying goodbye to Nia too. She is exasperating, unruly, and tries my patience daily, yet without her, the corners of my life, those reserved especially for dogs, are empty again.

24

_____

SPIDERS AND SNAKES

I SUFFER a slight panic attack not long after Charlie leaves.
It's the middle of the night. Not wanting to alarm Sarah, I
wake her and announce that I am going to the hospital. In my
irrational state of mind, this makes perfect sense to me.

"Hey, I don't feel good," I announce as I stand in the
doorway of her bedroom, struggling desperately to place a left
shoe on my right foot. I don't mention the painful, red bite
mark on my hand that I received earlier in the day while
hoisting a bale of hay. I don't tell her that the pain has been
traveling up my arm, which is now numb and tingling. I don't
explain that I am convinced I have suffered the bite of a
poisonous snake or brown recluse spider, but *what other
explanation can there be?*

I have painstakingly researched the Internet for the past
few hours, comparing photos and reading symptoms while
applying ice packs and topical ointments. Anti-
inflammatories are not working. My symptoms now include a
headache and stomach ache. I am weak, dizzy, sweating, and

feel as though I may vomit. My throat tightening and the pressure in my chest becoming unbearable, I hurry to get dressed, and then I brush my teeth. *Who cares about their breath in an emergency?* I do it anyway.

Convinced, now, that I have only hours left for the hospital to locate and transport the antivenom that I will need for survival, I say a quick goodbye to Sarah. She rolls over in her bed, one eye open. "Okay." Having witnessed this scenario countless times, she is unfazed. "Have a good trip," she mumbles.

I am off. Hours later, having received the needed reassurance from the doctors that the bite is nothing, that the problem is in my head and not my arm, I arrive home in time to wake her for school.

By springtime, the barn has endured such a rigorous cleaning that it appears no horses actually live in it, clearly an effort to ward off my new obsession with snakes and spiders.

"You realize that those things can get in the house too, right?" Sarah admonishes me.

I raise my hands in mock surrender. "Please. I can only deal with one psychosis at a time." I tell her.

The horses are crazed with new energy from the fresh grasses, and we can barely keep them contained. They kick up their heels in the pasture and, when allowed the freedom of the yard, they circle the house like madmen. Sarah's laughter fills the rooms as thunderous hooves streak past our front door and again past the kitchen window. Later that afternoon, a relaxing trail ride will become a race between Sarah and me to the finish line, which is really just the end of our dead-end road.

I hear nothing about the foreclosure proceedings in Austin. The boys seem in a perpetual state of denial, making no effort to consider a solution—their existence complacent, continuous, never-ending.

I have plenty to occupy my time, but gradually thoughts of Charlie creep into my head. I have not heard from him in... how long? Has it really been months? No. I can't possibly have gone that long without calling. He would have called me if he needed anything. No news is good news. Everything's fine.

I try to break free from my thoughts, but eventually, I give in. Curling up on the couch one evening, I reach for my phone.

"Hi. How's everything?" I ask when his voice comes on the line.

"Good," he responds. "Things are good."

"Any news on the house?"

"Nope." It is all he offers.

The house! I want to shout. The one that will soon be pulled out from under the three of you! Make plans! Do something! Though, even if I scream it, I know he will not hear.

I change the subject. We talk for a while about mundane things. When he doesn't share any news about Nia, I ask about her too. "How's she doing?" I brace myself for the worst. Is he taking care of her? Does he still have her? Would he tell me if he didn't?

And then, "She's fine." A pause. "I took her to a park."

"To a park? That's great." Progress. This is progress.

"Yeah," he answers. "She has a fit when she wants to go

out. Drives me crazy. Once, I thought she was actually gonna open the door by herself."

I am well aware of how annoyingly persistent Nia can be. This is exactly what I had hoped for. Nia is doing her job— her irritating, full speed ahead, know no boundaries job.

"And the others? Do they like her?" Is anyone else benefiting from her neediness? Do they ever wake up? Do they set foot outside?

"I guess," he answers in his usual non-committal, non-informative way.

I don't push for details. Nia has been to a park. Charlie has gone outside. The issue with the house seems stagnant, for now. There's some light.

I sigh. There is still such a long way to go.

25

INTERNET

I MAINTAIN a love-hate relationship with the Internet. An amazing benefit to introverts like me, it is also an incredible source of too much information. When I am in full panic mode, I should stay away from it. On the plus side, it has facilitated my independent lifestyle, enabling me to fix household plumbing problems, lay an entire bathroom tile floor, and rebuild my lawn mower. Considering that I would rather poke myself in the eye than ask for help, it is possibly my most valuable resource.

It had also been my lifeline when Charlie was in the military, offering a static connection to his wanderings—but I am no longer obsessed with military websites. I am concerned about the thousands of young men who are still overseas, but I know where *my* boys are. They are out of danger, or are they? Their detachment weighs on my mind as usual, and the computer seems a good opportunity to check on them.

I log on, scanning Instagram accounts and Facebook profiles for updates that might indicate healthy activity or interests. I have scanned before, and as usual, see nothing on Charlie's timeline besides pre-military posts. I search for Grant. No luck there. And then success. I come across a grainy video newly posted on James' page and enlarge the screen for a closer look. The empty living room comes into view, the fireplace now supporting the training dummy. Leaning wearily against the red brick, he sports a tattered T-shirt. A pair of broken sunglasses hang from his head. It appears he has lost his final battle. The grill is now abutted directly against the patio door, allowing easy access that probably borders on a fire hazard.

Suddenly, there is James in the video, walking into the frame, taking a seat cross-legged on the floor and then, Nia, fluttering around him like some enormous firefly, darting in and out of the screen, brushing her nose against his shoulder, jumping back, challenging him to play.

I watch James place an assortment of plastic cups upside-down on the floor in front of him. Like an old magic trick, he hides a ball underneath one of the cups and rearranges them. As though a light switch has been thrown, the flickering animal stops, mesmerized by the cups before her. Drawing her in, James speaks with a low and steady voice, instructing her not to touch until he gives the command. Her head lowers, her mouth closes. When the command comes, Nia extends her paw, touching the cup that holds the ball. Success! James praises her lavishly as Nia wriggles and squirms her delight, then she settles while he rearranges the cups again.

On a second try, he gently reprimands her when she stands and attempts to use her nose as a pointer. Quickly, she resumes the more acceptable pawing technique. She is right every time, no matter how he rearranges them. Perhaps it's the scent of the ball, though a treat would surely entice her more. At a casual glance, it appears she is intent on the placement of the cups, but there is more going on here. I blink my eyes and zoom in closer on the dog. Nia clearly sees the cups, but she is observing James. His subtle hand movement, the tone of his voice, a slight inclination of head and shoulders that I'm not sure even he notices, she is taking it in. Maybe it's just me, but Nia's success seems to be not in watching the ball, but in reading her companion.

Sitting on the floor in the room, just him and the dog—James looks ragged, unshaven, and unwashed—his hair wildly astray, his clothes hanging off his frame. Ordinarily, the sight would dismay me, yet as I watch him enthusiastically praise her for each correct trick, like a child, ecstatic over her success, as pleased with himself as with her, I feel a whisper of hope.

The video replays in my head for the rest of the day. I know the boys aren't making progress other than their occasional visits to the park. Their military pay, which they had little use for during their active duty, will eventually run out and, without jobs, there will be no way to pay the utilities or buy food. It is possible that they may never fully adjust? Unable to participate in life and with seemingly limited connection to family and friends, they are missing birthdays, graduations, holidays, sunsets, rain, cool breezes. Dating, marriage, and possibly children seem destined for others, not them. Life passes by just outside their door, the door that they will open only wide enough for pizza.

But then there is Nia, working relentlessly each day to keep them engaged, reminding them of small accomplishments, enabling them to feel moments of pride, gently nudging them back to life. The beauty of the dog lies not only in what she gives but also in what she doesn't give. Nia makes no judgment or criticism, brings no pressure or deadlines, and communicates without speaking a word.

I try to send my thoughts to James. *Take a shower. Get dressed. Open the door.* Such an easy thing, yet so extraordinarily difficult for them. Thank God Nia can fit through the crack.

26

TOO MUCH INFORMATION

"You're really knowledgeable about this stuff," a coworker reflects after inquiring about a particular medical condition. Having explained the most common characteristics of the illness, types of diagnostic tools readily available, options for treatment and, of course, specific warning signs to watch for, I nod half-heartedly and force a smile.

"Thanks," I tell her. "Glad I could help."

"That's what hypochondriacs live for," I mumble, frantically sterilizing my desk with disinfectant wipes as she walks away.

It's a big office. No cubicles here. Desk after desk line the cavernous seventh floor of the courthouse, home to forty maybe more, busy worker bees. Down here, the focus is on the quantity of work, curiously more so than the quality. Supervisors discourage conversation, which I like. When I am not upstairs in the courtrooms, I am here, making every effort to shrink myself into the corners, and yet somehow I have become the go-to person for health questions. It never ceases to amaze me that people seek me out for medical advice. Who would want my advice when I'm the one who needs help? I shake my head, shift position in my chair, and redirect my thoughts to the project at hand.

While my days revolve around work, chores, and Sarah's activities, my nights center around my own health. Late at night, without distractions, I focus solely on my imaginary symptoms. No surprise, focusing makes them worse.

To those of us prone to panic attacks, easy access to too much information—TV, radio, books, newspapers, the Internet, especially the Internet—only adds to our nightmares. The more you search, the more you find—and I am a master at finding things that I was not aware existed, but describe me perfectly. My use of such a powerful tool should be medically regulated or better yet, forbidden given my inability to control the urge to look.

In the early hours, left to my own devices in a panic-stricken and sleep-deprived state, I can diagnose myself with every conceivable ailment known to man, even if I can't pronounce it or it doesn't exist within our borders. If the sickness is rare or eradicated by modern medicine, the inability of the doctors to correctly diagnose it seems justified.

Of course, they don't know what it is. No one has seen it in over one hundred years, until now, until me.

27

AUSTIN

In July I am back in Austin for another weekend, negotiating traffic in another rental car while heading towards a Texas-size store. Charlie occupies the passenger seat next to me. The store is an outdoorsman's dream. I had mentioned the grill and smoker section in an effort to lure him out of the house. If that failed to entice him, my backup was the guns and ammo department. Though he hesitated at first, he agreed to go.

During the drive, I access the number of the Veterans Administration, pre-set on my cell phone. I haven't asked if it is okay with Charlie. I don't care if he has an opinion. Time is moving on. I am determined to move him forward, and here he is, seated in the passenger seat with no way to escape. He doesn't say a word. He sits, staring straight ahead, arms crossed much like an angry child, but he makes no effort to stop me.

Ten minutes into the ride, the call connects, and I'm placed on hold. Minutes pass as I drive under the speed limit, trying to stretch the time. The occasional horn honk doesn't deter me. I'm in the slow lane after all, and I am not pulling over for this call lest Charlie should make a break for it. Inevitably, we arrive at the store where we wait, engine running. Neither of us says a word.

Come on. Tension builds inside me, the clock on the dash ticking off the seconds so loudly now, it screams. In this fragile moment, trying to connect the two, Charlie and the VA, I fear the opportunity may be lost forever. I consider engaging the car again as I survey the parking lot. It's huge and practically empty. I could do ninety in this thing. That would keep him in. But I am too nervous to move.

Please don't get out of the car. I silently will Charlie to stay.

Please answer the phone, I plead wordlessly with the entire entity that is the Veterans Administration, though even as I sit in silent agony, I know that my thoughts are futile. I may have initiated the action, but I am powerless over the outcome.

As the minute's pass, doubt creeps in. For all of my best intentions, I can't force Charlie to get help any more than I can keep him inside the vehicle. This is not his only avenue—it's just the one that I am pursuing. He may be tolerating my method, but he is not a willing participant. He has already made that clear, I simply refuse to listen, only proving that I can be just as stubborn as my son.

We sit in silence for fourteen agonizing minutes, my mind teetering between painful acceptance and the terrifying possibility of failure, when, at long last, I hear a voice on the other end. I quickly gather my thoughts and ask to make an appointment.

"It's not actually for me," I explain.

The voice apologizes, cites something about privacy and explains that the service member will have to supply the required information.

"Of course." I sigh.

Here it is—the roadblock I had anticipated. I can go no further. I have to accept that Charlie will take the steps he needs to get better when he is ready and not before. The VA may never be his chosen path, no matter how slow or fast I drive.

As he is suggesting convenient times to call back, I lay the phone down on the console for a moment to remove the keys from the ignition (I'm right-handed. I have no choice). The voice on the phone continues. Charlie can listen if he wants—there is nothing more I can do. Defeated, I gather my purse, unlatch my seatbelt, and struggle to locate the door handle.

"Saturdays can be extremely busy. Monday mornings seem to be the best time to get through. We would be glad to..."

Charlie picks up the phone.

Interrupting the representative in mid-sentence, he identifies himself. In a few moments, he is supplying his DD214 information firmly yet politely, as though some unspoken command has been given, and he has an obligation to comply. The call is quick and precise. Charlie answers some questions, gives some information, jots down instructions. He ends the brief conversation with, "Yes, sir.

Thank you, sir," and gently places the phone back onto the console.

Though I don't say a word, the significance of the milestone does not escape me. Almost two years in the making, it is done. He will be scheduled for an assessment with the doctors at his local Veterans Administration Health Center. The appointment information and necessary paperwork will be sent in the mail.

I feel something different about the exchange, a delicate shift in our connection. In my resolve to lay down the torch, Charlie had continued the quest. We sit in silent solidarity for a moment, both of us having reached out to this nameless, faceless person on the phone. After a lifetime of contention, it seems there is simply no more fight left in either of us.

We exit the car and Charlie follows me into the store. As we peruse the aisles, I notice perspiration beginning to dot his T-shirt. Though he is eye level with the merchandise, he searches higher, fixating on the exit signs. I try to engage him in conversation, directing him toward the creative displays and the expansive inventory. There is no response.

To our left, elk, moose, and caribou balance on faux rock formations that extend to the second floor; the taxidermy figures available for closer inspection if one chooses to ride the escalator. To our right, an entire camping village beckons us to scrutinize tents and consider cots. I've never seen anything like it and, though I am personally astounded, Charlie's mind is somewhere else. I resist the urge to ask if he is all right. He isn't. I quickly cut the shopping trip short, an easy maneuver considering that every aisle I turn down he follows closely behind.

"There's not really much in here," I remark, observing the football field of outdoor inventory before me. "Let's go." Charlie practically trips over me on the way out.

Back inside the car, he wipes the sweat that trickles down his face and adjusts the air conditioning vent to blow directly on him. The tension in his body eases, his breathing slows. As he relaxes again on the ride back to the house, I am certain that we have just narrowly avoided a panic attack. I would know.

A lot of triggers can affect soldiers. The sudden slamming of a door, the crack of a tree limb, debris in the road—any of these can easily startle a veteran, even cause a flashback. I am not sure what prompted Charlie's discomfort in the store. Too many people? Too loud? No escape? What you resist persists. To make progress, the boys have to expose themselves to the very things that they choose to avoid. I make a mental note to try another store, another day, perhaps during another trip to Texas.

The next evening, he speaks about it. To my wonder, he tries to explain. I had lightly suggested a future outing. As far as Charlie was concerned, there would be no more.

"Well, just think about it," I had stated after his refusal.

Sitting in the living room with me, the others in their bedrooms, Charlie struggles to verbalize his feelings. Perhaps he feels he owes some defense. It catches me off guard that he is willing to talk. I'm sitting cross-legged at one end of the futon. Charlie is at the other. Nia stretches lazily between us, a giant furry connection, her head in my lap, her hind feet poking Charlie while she sleeps. I hadn't intended to pressure him for an explanation, only to encourage another outing. I am surprised at his words, even more so that he is saying them to me.

Intensified, personal—these are the words that he uses. Every small thing seems magnified, he explains. He stares vacantly across the room as he talks. That minor transgression by the store clerk in St. Louis, when he was newly discharged and beginning his drive to Austin, was anything but minor in his mind. Standing there at the counter, the wait had seemed excruciatingly long, igniting a burning rage inside him. During that same drive to Texas, he suffered a flat tire. The sound of the tire bursting sent him into fight mode, hastily reaching for his gun while struggling to maintain control of the vehicle on the highway. More incidents occurred along the way, other triggers. A car, driving too closely next to his, set off alarms in his head, putting him on high alert. A casual look by a fellow motorist was a personal offense, though he tried to tell himself otherwise.

He felt more comfortable in Iraq with fellow Marines by his side than he did in the civilian world. By the time he reached Austin, he was a wreck, wired, and on edge—emotionally exhausted from the trip. Fearing that he might be unable to control his reactions, that he would act inappropriately or dangerously, he resigned himself to staying inside the house. Upon his arrival, he realized that James and Grant were doing the same thing.

"That's extremely responsible," I say softly. "To remove yourself from situations until you get better."

He turns his head to gaze at me, his eyes so sad I think *I* may cry. Nia sighs deeply in my lap. Charlie turns away.

28

MORE THERAPY

AFTER MY CANCER diagnosis and subsequent treatments, *worrier* had been my motto—not to be confused with *warrior* by any stretch of the imagination. I agonized over every injection, every surgery, every treatment. It was a wonder I absorbed anything the doctors said.

I never escaped that worry, not when the treatments were over, not even after many years had passed. The possibility that dangerous cells still inhabited my body continued to haunt me. Eventually, added stressors contributed to my lack of mental restraint, pushing me to anxiety attacks.

Unexplained pain can send me frantically searching for a diagnosis, which I fervently argue to the ER doctors is accurate and in need of remedy. My co-pay is one hundred dollars, which I gladly fork over. Professional perspective is priceless. It is my therapy. Even without insurance I would not have been deterred; penniless and poverty-stricken, yes—but not deterred.

My method is irrational, of course, fueled by my

dysfunctional imagination. Even if my cancer returned, my worst fear of all, the emergency room is not the place to stop it. Cancers are slow-growing and slowly treated evils. All the doctors and nurses in the ER are not capable of miraculously curing a patient and sending them home the same day. What I really want is the reassurance that my fear is irrational. I need to hear the words, spoken with authority and perhaps confirmed by an appropriate number of tests. I *need* to know that I am wasting their time.

There is one other thing that helps. When I am in Texas with the boys, focusing on their recovery, I am not focusing on myself. Upon my return to Florida, the anxieties surface again. A strange way to work out my own problems, perhaps, but my trips to Texas are helping me. The boys pull me out of my carefully controlled world. Administering to their needs requires cars, airports, planes, people, and travel. In light of their steadfast reluctance to leave the house, I see no other choice. Being with them requires that I present myself as a healthy, levelheaded individual in my efforts to lead by example. Determined to help them, I am forced to move past my own insecurities.

One dark weekend, I lie on my couch at home, my head throbbing from a minor injury earlier in the day—never attempt to stand abruptly while your head is still in a cabinet. Some would argue that I should wear a helmet on a daily basis. Now an ice pack is strapped to my head with two ribbons and a bungee cord (all I could find). Even tied down, it keeps shifting, regardless, and I am reluctant to make even the slightest movement. My head throbs from the effort it takes to hold it still.

It's probably minor of course, but as usual, I have imagined it into something far more sinister. For the last two hours, I have worked myself into a state of worry. The only blessing: I cannot reach for my phone to look up possible complications of head injuries as doing so would involve moving my head. If I were in Texas with the boys, I would minimize a situation like this in an effort not to stress *them* out.

Sarah has long since retired for the night, irritated with my complaints and unable to watch a movie without my constant interruptions. Immune as she is to my self-imposed misery, she has simply waved it off and gone to bed. It's late. I'm afraid to sleep, now alone with the possibility that I may not wake up.

In this pitiful state, afraid to move, afraid to sleep, afraid of what, I'm not even sure, I try to review the symptoms of concussion in my mind, particularly the medical criteria that distinguish *mild* from *severe*. I focus on signs of deterioration, a clue, a symptom, something that will cue me that it is time to *go to the hospital*. Though my eyelids are heavy, I resist sleep. If only someone else could keep watch while I rest.

In my misery, it dawns on me that I would prefer to lie in a hospital bed, hooked up to monitors and observed continuously by medical professionals for the rest of my life, just in case something goes wrong.

The thought quite literally opens my eyes. It is my lowest point, and it scares me. Lying there on my sofa in the dark, bungee cord strapped to my head, I realize that the security I crave is the most frightening prospect of all. My imagined scenario means that my entire life, not only my health, would be out of my control. I have truly imagined myself into a prison, one that I may be destined to live if I can't imagine myself out of it.

What kind of life would that be? Isn't the notion of extreme self-preservation what I am trying to prevent in Texas? There is a point when taking measures to live in a safe environment hinders the ability to lead a healthy life.

The four of us, me and the boys, are all walking a slippery slope, one that is too close to the hazy edge of a cliff. In what only I would perceive as a risky move, I roll over on the sofa to a more comfortable position, let the ice pack fall to the floor and wait for sleep, firm in my decision that on Monday I will make an appointment with a new therapist.

29

TIME CRUNCH

Grant gets a job. GRANT GETS A JOB! He begins installing windows. It is backbreaking, physical work made even more arduous by the hot Texas sun. His brother had reached out to him for assistance, and he accepted. A work truck picks him up in the early morning and returns him, filthy and exhausted, in the late afternoon. We stand in silent recognition. In my mind, I can see him gazing out of the truck window, passing pieces of a world he has not seen in over a year. Upon arrival home, he promptly showers, puts on his robe, and retreats to his room. I am beside myself. I am ecstatic. *This* is progress.

To employ a veteran seems, to me, to tap into a gold mine. Most veterans I have met are polite and self-sufficient, honor authority figures, think globally, and bypass the trivial or trendy. There are many reasons to hire these men and women who have undergone intense physical and mental training and reflect the values of a soldier. Even though soldiers admit they "feel different" and "feel like they don't fit in," they are different in positive ways. Emotionally mature, goal-oriented, mission-driven, experienced leaders, they know the value of teamwork. They not only understand the concept of sacrifice for the greater good, but they have also lived it. Struggles aside, their differences set them apart from others in many wonderful ways. Grant's employment is good news, not only for him but for some employer out there who will soon realize what a priceless resource he has gained.

Upon contacting the realtor a second time, the boys receive an extension to vacate the house. December 31 will be the final date. It is now almost September. The reprieve puts a new demand on their recovery. They need to make some serious plans. Along with their dwindling finances, in four months they will be out of a place to live. Even with the grace of the extension, they are truly running out of time.

30

GONE

Later that month, I am sitting at my desk at work taking stock of various courtroom exhibits. Spread before me is an array of objects: hundreds of handwritten notes, stacks of financial statements, photos of children caught in the middle of a mess, a tarnished and stained kitchen knife—the significance of which I am not entirely certain. It's not a murder trial I am monitoring, at least not yet. Each individual item entered into evidence in the courtroom must be cataloged and secured, to be returned to the rightful owners only by court order. I am just getting settled in when my desk phone rings. Charlie is on the other end.

"Mom?"

He never calls me on my work phone. I was not aware that he even knew the number. Concern immediately envelops me. "Everything okay?" I brace myself.

He gets straight to the point. "Nia's gone."

"Gone, as in...?" I can't even form the rest of the words.

Gone, as in what? Gone for a walk? Gone for a day? Gone forever? My mind races with scenarios.

"A hole under the fence in the yard," he continues. "She got out. And she hasn't come back."

"When?"

"I let her out last night. She didn't come back in." Charlie sounds slightly panicked.

"Okay. Relax," I hear myself say. "Where have you looked for her? Did you cover the neighborhood?"

No response.

"Have you talked with the neighbors? Maybe someone has seen her."

Silence on the other end.

"Charlie? Are you still there?"

The response comes back quietly. "I've been watching out the window for her."

It dawns on me that he won't go outside, not without the dog.

"Where is Grant? Where is James?"

"James is here," Charlie answers. "He's watching the back. I'm watching the front." I end the call with a combination of hopeful words and suggestions of where she might be. I ponder the irony. Nia is their lifeline, giving them the ability to move around freely outdoors, and now Nia is gone. Searching for her, without her, is not an option.

I contemplate the dilemma. I am in Florida. The boys aren't leaving the house. Is it possible that I may have to book a flight to hunt for her myself? That could be a while, and time is a major factor. Could I organize a search party when I don't know anyone in Texas other than the boys? And just how would I explain the situation, even if I did have someone to contact?

Would you please look for their dog, because they are unable to?

I'm stuck, at least for the time being. I try to concentrate on the massive project before me, but the problem weighs on my mind for the rest of the day. Thankfully, no one notices my distraction or cares that the inventory is not close to completion by the end of the day. My coworkers are just grateful they don't have to do it.

When I arrive home that evening a message blinks on my answering machine. I push the button hoping for good news. It is, sort of. It's a veterinary office in Texas.

"Someone may have found your dog," says a female voice on the recorder. "Please call."

Relieved, I punch the number into my phone, anxiously tapping the kitchen countertop as I wait for an answer.

"Someone brought her in," the receptionist tells me a few minutes later. "We scanned her for a microchip. She has one, but it wasn't registered. So we called the shelter that issued it. They checked their records and gave us your name. It took some detective work, but we found your number."

I thank her and say I will call the boys to come get her.

"She's not here," the woman explains.

My heart sinks.

"The person who found her gave her to someone else, and that guy brought her in for identification. We couldn't keep her here, so he took her home. Let me try to find his contact information and call you back."

I pace the tile floor, waiting for the information. I'm

hesitant to call Charlie until I am sure we'll be getting
the dog.

What if they can't reach this guy? What if he refuses to
give her back? No, he wouldn't have bothered to have her
scanned, would he?

Finally, the call comes through. They now have a name
and address. "Will that help?" she asks. I tell her it will and
thank her profusely. The address is just three houses down
from the boys and, hopefully, the neighbor still has Nia.

This time, mustering all the conviction in my voice that I
can, I tell Charlie that he *has* to go down the street and get
her. She *is not* going to walk home by herself. She isn't far.
Nia is waiting for him.

"Okay," says Charlie, a slight catch of relief in his voice.

Armed with the address and cloaked by darkness, he and
James leave the house together to retrieve their canine
lifeline.

31

THE LIBRARY

I WANT to understand the trauma that affects so many of our veterans. I need to understand. Researching my own medical issues consumes a good portion of my life. I can at least research something more useful, something that might actually help someone. My focus turns to PTSD.

The Mayo Clinic defines post-traumatic stress disorder as a mental health condition triggered by a terrifying event—either experiencing it or witnessing it. Though not limited to combat vets, we commonly associate the term with our returning soldiers.

Recognized in early World War I, symptoms at the time were often referred to as "shell shock." In World War II, the shell shock diagnosis was replaced by "combat stress reaction." Other names have included battle scars, stress syndrome, battle fatigue, and traumatic war neurosis. It wasn't until the 1980s that The American Psychiatric Association added PTSD to the third edition of its *Diagnostic and Statistical Manual of Mental Disorders.*

My yearning to know more prompts an additional stop to my commute. Sarah and I make a visit to our public library. Sarah socializes with friends more than she browses the books but manages to finish some summer reading, regardless. I scrutinize my new destination. I haven't been to a library in years.

The place is old and shaped somewhat like a wheel—each category branching off from a small rotunda. Metal rolling carts dot the aisles, overflowing with publications waiting to be shelved. The timeworn building with faded wallpaper and worn carpet needs renovation—but it is still vital and wise in its contents.

I carve out a corner in the psychology section and surround myself with books, strategically taking more than I can read, stacking them like little towers around me as I sit on the floor, a makeshift effort to avoid social interaction.

PTSD is characterized by difficulty concentrating, anxiety, paranoia, withdrawal, avoidance, flashbacks, irritability, anger, physical restlessness, nightmares, avoidance of stimuli associated with the trauma, increased arousal—such as difficulty falling asleep, hypervigilance, memory disturbances, and thoughts of suicide.

I had watched my father, a veteran of World War II, struggle with what I now recognize as PTSD, although it wasn't something that we talked about in my family. As far as I know, he never sought treatment for it. My father was a kind man, but I remember him as distant and anxious, lavishing affection on his dogs more than his children. He was guarded and quiet like Charlie is now.

Guarded? Quiet? Sitting in the corner, avoiding eye

contact with passersby, flinching when someone wanders too close or, even worse, appears as though they may try to engage me in conversation, I recognize myself in the diagnosis.

PTSD often begins within one to three months of a traumatic event, although some symptoms may not begin until years later. Early intervention reduces the chance that the stress reaction will become chronic PTSD. If treatment is delayed, veterans often develop unhealthy coping strategies—yet many of our returning veterans simply don't have the opportunity for treatment. They must not only find employment but also put back together torn families and lives, with little time to work through their emotional baggage.

I try to imagine a smooth transition from soldier to civilian. What is needed, in my view, is a mandatory decompression period, one where all soldiers would check into a rehabilitation facility on their base before returning home.

In my scenario, every soldier would be required to participate in this decompression period. Treatment would be lengthy, three-to-six months, possibly longer; never less. Healing of the mind typically cannot begin until the service member is no longer receiving danger signals and the brain's chemistry normalizes. This can take months, even years. Each soldier should at least be offered a solid start, whether they feel they need it or not.

They would attend mandatory individual and group counseling. Medications would be administered if necessary. Exercise would be monitored, and sleep cycles regulated.

Soldiers would learn what symptoms to watch for and receive contact information for follow-up treatments.

This transition period would be written into their contracts and included in their service requirement. It would not extend their service but would be a necessary part of it. Future job and housing information would be made available. Physical health would be evaluated. The ultimate goal, of course, would be to resume civilian life acclimated, aware of the difficulties that may lie ahead and reassured that the government stands behind them in their transition.

Adjusting my position, I draw my legs underneath me. Sarah waves from across the room. I return her wave with a smile. Except for occasional muffled giggles from her teen section, it's quiet in here. It's the library, after all. The aroma of old books, coupled with strategically placed rocking chairs radiates a warmth that reminds me of my grandmother's house so many years ago. Should a grandfather clock chime, I would not be the least bit surprised.

My dad was Charlie's age when he returned to my grandmother's home after his service. Did she notice a difference in him at the time? Did she have any resources with which to help him? He eventually became employed, married, and had children, luckily for me, but I know none of it was easy for him. Those who have not worked through their own psychological trauma can profoundly affect the people closest to them. If problems go untreated, one is at a higher risk of domestic violence, substance abuse, and poor work history.

It has been such a long time now for Charlie, James, and Grant, sitting inside the house in Austin with no therapeutic intervention. In their defense, the boys have established their own respite period with their self-imposed isolation, and they *are* making a little progress. But with no significant forward movement and no effective treatment, their stagnant state is potentially irreversible.

In the next aisle, a service dog, a yellow lab, lies quietly while his owner browses. His velvety muzzle appears to melt into the tan carpet as a soft exhale escapes from the side of his lip. His presence reminds me of another important tool for recovery. I am not a psychologist, nor am I am qualified to challenge the workings of our military. I fully concede there is much I don't know. I do, however, make a case for a dog.

In my imagined scenario, every returning soldier would be encouraged to connect with a credible service dog organization and learn the benefits of owning such a dog. Studies have shown that interacting and caring for a dog can reduce blood pressure, increase physical activity, relieve anxiety and depression, increase focus, attention skills and self-esteem, and elevate mood. Canine therapy can teach people to manage their emotions. One of the greatest benefits of therapy dogs is the increase of endorphins, a neurotransmitter in the brain that functions similarly to opiate drugs—a natural substance produced by the body that manipulates the perception of pain or stress. Animals can boost happiness, improve empathy, and promote a happier life.

This is marginal, some might say, compared to clinical therapeutic efforts that may be used to help bring a soldier to a healthier mental state. Yet, each dynamic offers one more possibility, and each soldier may respond to one form of therapy more readily than to another. For many veterans, canine companionship has proven to be a key factor in their recovery.

For the three veterans in Texas, an alliance has been made, and the connection is not through a psychologist, therapist, doctor, or the government. There, in that dark, cold house with shut doors and drawn curtains—where I am desperately trying to assist in fighting a private battle against the fallout of emotional trauma—my partner and ally in this mission is a dog. Scoff at the observation if you will, but amazingly, what seemed at first only a vague possibility, is working. It is a dog that, for the last eight months has been steadily laying the groundwork of trust and providing a foundation for these damaged young men to begin to live, really live, again.

32

MICE

Sarah accompanies me on my next trip to Austin. She's been back in school only a week, but its Labor Day weekend and the frequent flyer is happy for the quick getaway. Her optimism eases the stress of travel for me and adds a dimension of cheerfulness to the house. Initially somewhat timid in her presence, the boys soon warm to her lively company, and they laugh and talk well into the night.

The next morning, Charlie retires to one of the back bedrooms. Grant has gone off to work. Sarah is sleeping in the *gun room*, as I call it, after warning her not to so much as put her foot on the carpet or her hand on the wall, in case the arsenal now barricaded in the closet should miraculously come alive.

I am attempting to clean the small kitchen while James stands like a statue in the middle of the room. We have established a working relationship, he and I. He is the most willing to pitch in around the house, and is now trying to assist in some way, though, perhaps, isn't quite sure how. At least that's what I assume until I notice the large butcher knife in his hand and realize he is on the lookout for mice. I don't want to think about the outcome should he see one of the errant rodents.

Mice have taken over the kitchen; indeed, the whole house. Quite alarmed, I had procured a precautionary prescription for antibiotics upon my first visit. Droppings can be seen on the countertops, on the bathroom tiles, and in the closets. Mice pop out everywhere—a hole in the bathroom wall, the fireplace in the living room. Cooking is probably not a good idea, but cleaning is—and right now, I'm doing the best I can—armed with thick plastic gloves and a disinfectant spray bottle while James stands at attention, waiting to fight off any possible intruders.

Nia stretches out on the floor between us, enjoying the cool tile and the company until something about James' demeanor awakens her curiosity. Suddenly, her eyes are fixed on him. Like a tiger, she quietly rises to join him in his watch, her front end crouching as though ready to pounce.

When a small gray mouse appears from behind the stove and scurries across the countertop, I scream. James lunges for the mouse with his knife, but Nia is quicker, leaping across the kitchen in a blur of brown, slapping both front feet on the counter. Before James even has a chance, she turns her head sideways and scoops the mouse into her jaws, dragging her nails across the Formica countertop, knocking my cleaning supplies to the floor. She runs out of the kitchen with her prey—tiny bones crunching between her teeth.

James calls out to her as she disappears. "Good girl! Good Nia!"

In a moment she pops back into the room, jaws smacking, satisfied, and ready for her next conquest. If I had entertained *any* thoughts of cooking, they are gone now. I continue my efforts to clean, but I am firm in my decision that a home-cooked meal is simply not on the menu.

Gathering my supplies, I return to tackling the microwave while James retreats to the living room. Sitting on the carpet, he calls Nia to him, and through the window, I watch him interact with her. He sits cross-legged, pieces of dry dog food in a small pile to his left, dog toys surrounding him. Nia stands in front of him.

The training dummy appears to be watching as well, leaning slightly forward, his head now inexplicably wrapped in cellophane. The damn thing continues to catch me off guard, and I still jump each time I enter the room. I hate the *man,* though I keep my decorating opinions to myself.

"Sit," he tells her in a soft voice, and she obeys. "Shake. Speak. Lie down. Roll over." I watch James gently command the dog's attention, and Nia quickly falls under his spell, suddenly so still she barely breathes. His patience and quiet way amaze me as the two work effortlessly together. Nia's keen eye never wavers; she's ready for his slightest movement or quietest command. So precise are their movements—they seem to read each other's thoughts. With a nod, he instructs her to pick up a stray dishtowel. At the slightest motion of his hand, she obediently drops it in his lap.

Focused and eager to please, Nia no longer exhibits the unruliness of the puppy that had single-handedly destroyed most of my Florida home, causing me, at times, to question her adoption. Here, in the living room with James, they appear to be of the same mindset, both intrigued by the challenges before them and connected in their efforts to communicate.

I set the spray bottle on the countertop and tiptoe to the edge of the room to get a closer look, careful not to distract them, though that seems an impossibility. The house could be burning down, and they would remain fixated only on each other. James lifts two dirty plastic cups. Nia's ears perk forward with excitement. I have seen this trick in his Facebook video. I stretch my neck to get a better view. James glances up at me, then regains his focus. He places a treat under one of the cups and shifts them both in circles on the carpet. Nia waits for permission, motionless. Seconds tick by. James is still. I am still. The tension is almost unbearable.

Then, "Where is it?" he asks the dog, his voice more urgent now, and she extends her right paw toward the correct cup. "Good girl!" James jumps up from the floor, clapping and bouncing like a cheerleader. Nia springs up to meet him.

"You're really good with her," I tell him when they have settled again.

"She's a smart dog."

"Did you have a dog when you were growing up?"

"No." James looks at the floor and rolls a cup toward the dog. I watch it circle just out of reach of Nia's extended paw and try to imagine growing up without dogs.

"Have you ever worked with dogs?" I am curious to know where his patience and technique with the animal has originated.

"No. Well, there was this dog in Iraq..." His voice drops. "We called him Ham. He helped me, well, all of us, kind of

get through our days. I worked with him when I could."
James trails his hand across the carpeted floor. Nia follows it
with her eyes. "He sort of got your mind off of... stuff. That
dog was pretty quick at learning too."

The conversation may be superficial, the training just a
game, but I am intrigued. While Charlie and Grant act gentle
and affectionate in their interactions with Nia, James has
tapped into a connection with the dog that encompasses far
more than companionship. The two share a subtle
understanding, a connection of minds between man and
animal. He has grasped her way of thinking and, in doing so,
has developed a deeper way of communicating with her.

Impressed with his quiet but firm demeanor as he
continues to work with Nia, I suggest, "You should be a dog
trainer."

James glances up, his face suddenly flushed.

Have I hit a nerve?

The idea is not new to me. The others have mentioned it,
as well, in reference to James. But, suddenly, it seems so
obvious to me that he should be moving in that direction,
channeling his talent and making it work for him.

I have more questions, but James has returned his
attention to the dog. Sensing I have made him uncomfortable,
I return to the kitchen, though from my distance, I observe
the living room training session. Nia and James are nose-to-
nose now. Stroking her silky ears, James has tuned out
everything but the dog. The boys jokingly refer to the stance
as "face-time," and I have witnessed each of them in deep
silences up close with Nia. James is in a safer place. Nia is in
her happiest place of all.

I spend the next morning at the grocery store, considering dogs, motivation, and possibilities. On my way back to the house, I spy a dog training facility in a strip mall. The name on the sign reads Zoom Room. It's open, despite the holiday. I pull into the parking lot and hesitate for a moment, mustering up the courage to go in.

Do it, I tell myself.

I close my eyes and visualize James sitting on the living room floor in January, the new owners of the house eyeing him suspiciously as they carry in their furnishings, careful not to step on him. The image is all the motivation I need. I open the door and exit the car.

Dressed in khakis and a shirt emblazoned with the company logo, a slender woman with long curly brown hair introduces herself as the owner and strikes up a conversation with me. Her name is Michelle.

I am struck by how comfortable I feel talking with this woman. Soon we are deep in conversation, our common interest in the animals connecting us with ease.

Clients and their dogs dot the room. It looks like a miniature gym with little mats and tiny orange traffic cones strewn about the area. A handful of participants attempt to navigate their pets over tiny jumps, across ramps, and through agility tunnels. Using hand signals and voice commands, their actions are animated and rarely successful. Other pet owners stand about, laughing, encouraging, and adding to the liveliness in the atmosphere.

Zoom Room is a franchise and a popular one, Michelle explains, especially during the winter months. Pet owners purchase memberships and use the facility for different levels of dog training from puppy socialization and obedience to certifications in higher training levels. Clients work with their pets under Michelle's direction or that of several other trainers.

Possibilities churn in my head as I shift the conversation toward James and Nia, recounting the way that they work together. Michelle offers her business card and says she would like to meet them. Before I leave, I have made an appointment for James. I breathe a sigh of relief. I've done it. But will he? I'll describe the place to him as best I can and hope for the best. Exposure to trainers and the chance to use all that equipment looks like it would be right up his alley, but if he won't leave the house... Well, I can only try.

We head back to Florida the next morning. On this visit, I have succeeded in getting the boys up and moving just enough to wash clothes, clean the house, and organize. It has been a busy, but happy, working weekend. Sarah's company has lightened the mood in the house. I have even opened the curtains. I fully expect they will close them as soon as we leave.

33

SERVICE DOGS

Many organizations specialize in matching veterans with dogs. I researched them with the thought that perhaps a specially trained dog could be even more helpful to the boys than Nia. Alas, most of these dogs are to be connected with *disabled* vets. Applications require a confirmed medical diagnosis. Therein lies the problem that the boys, and so many others like them, face. They have no medical diagnoses, have never sought treatment, suffer no obvious physical disability.

To gain access to these organizations that help veterans in need, the boys would first have to recognize their condition, seek out a medical professional, and actually talk about it to receive a diagnosis. As far as I can tell, they do not entirely view their desire to retreat from the world as a problem, much less a medical condition. There is much work to do before they can seek the help available to them—much less present an acceptable application for a service dog. In addition, if they refuse to be identified as disabled, they will refuse the assistance of a service dog that will advertise them as such.

Still, I don't take lightly the value of a trained service dog over Nia. At some later point, when the boys are more open to their circumstance, I might investigate the possibility again.

I abhor the popular practice of obtaining a service vest for an uncertified and untrained animal in an effort to bring a dog into an area that is commonly off limits. Adverse as the boys are to public places, Nia will never be found impersonating a service animal in the grocery store aisles or sitting by a table in a restaurant. She may be a different animal inside the house working with James, but outside, in the real world? I can imagine the scene—Nia bouncing down the aisles of the food store as if on springs, food flying off the shelves as she swats everything with that tail; or Nia in paradise, happily licking plates clean under some restaurant table. She is *not* a trained service dog.

I admit I have trouble with the term *emotional support dog,* separating certain dogs from the vast majority. Perhaps I am naïve, but aren't many dogs naturally supportive of their owners without special qualifications? Isn't that a large part of our bond with them?

Some dogs will never connect with humans; it's true. But, for many—given time, patience and opportunity—I would like to believe that the connection is there, under the surface, waiting to be discovered.

Nia's concern for the boys comes naturally to her. She

remains focused on each one, instinctively in tune to their demeanors. It is simply in her nature. It doesn't make her an "emotional support dog." It just makes her a dog, a dog with the right temperament, placed in the right home where the right healing can begin.

34

VETERANS ADMINISTRATION

A FEW WEEKS after our visit, Charlie informs me that he has kept his medical appointment at the VA. Having answered a few questions posed by a doctor during his physical exam, he is ushered down the hall to a therapist, with whom he speaks at length. He returns home with sample medication, pamphlets, written prescriptions, and appointments for future sessions.

"The doctor asked if I had trouble sleeping, if any situations caused anxiety, if I was doing okay with school or work," Charlie relates in his phone call later that evening. "I told him I wasn't in school and hadn't worked since I got out."

Good. Good that the doctor recognizes there might be a problem. And without an appointment, he was able to speak with a therapist? I thank the stars for mysteriously aligning. Getting Charlie back in another day may have proved difficult at best. All three boys negatively associate the VA with their military service. This appointment had been two months away, and I had feared that he would not attend. Yet he did. He kept the appointment, just as he had made the drive from Texas to Florida, fighting his demons along the way. I'm starting to feel like he is pulling himself out of this, and I anxiously await more improvements in his quality of life.

There are other avenues, but I feel strongly that the best help may come from other military members. The VA hospital, the last place they want to go, could be exactly where they need to be. Charlie has finally stepped through the doors. At the very least, it is an indication that he is ready to receive some help.

35

A LITTLE MORE TIME

LIFE CONTINUES for me and Sarah in Florida: work, school, work, horses, more work. The farm is a lot of work. In my off hours, I focus on safety features. One can never be too cautious. I hire someone to install electricity in the barn. When he is finished, I hire someone else to check his work. I install smoke and carbon monoxide detectors in the tack room. They go off randomly, scaring the poor horses who are now too frightened to approach the barn. Such things, I decide, are not really suitable for the outdoors.

Even with my challenges, or perhaps because of them, working with the horses is calming and restorative. I would argue that spending time with horses is equally as effective as professional help. Would I have sent a horse to Texas to help the boys? No, but I wouldn't be surprised if that form of therapy would have helped them as well.

The boys are always on my mind and one September Saturday, I fish Michelle's card from my wallet and hesitantly punch in the number for Zoom Room. She answers on the first ring. Reminding her of our previous conversation, I inquire whether James and Nia have come in.

"They have," she says, and I can't conceal my surprise.

"What do you think of them, the way they work together, the precision, the dedication, the patience?" It comes out as one long, breathless unstoppable sentence. In my exuberance, I may have blurted out, "Aren't they amazing?" though that would have been quite unlike me.

This is good news, and I am naively hopeful that a job offer may materialize for James. Michelle indicates that she was impressed with James and recommended that he come back to qualify for the Canine Good Citizen test, an obedience test recognized by the American Kennel Club.

Well, it's a start. Maybe James will be up for the challenge. After all, he had already stepped out the front door, driven fifteen minutes to Zoom Room and presented himself for the evaluation. Of course, Nia was by his side, proving a valuable partner in his first steps toward facing the world again.

In what becomes a quiet turning point of sorts, shortly after James' trip to Zoom Room, the perpetually solemn atmosphere in the house changes. I can tell even from my vantage point—twelve hundred miles away. James has been on a mission. He has returned unscathed and with confidence and news for the others about his success.

Until this time, *outdoors* for Nia has consisted mostly of opening the patio slider and allowing her unaccompanied access to the backyard and a few visits to the park on the corner. Now, the boys venture out of the house for short periods on their own, rather than in pairs, each one taking the dog with him. The change is as subtle as it is huge. Thereafter begins a gradual shift from absolute avoidance to more lengthy excursions, a shift one-and-a-half years in the making.

It isn't a smooth transition. There are days when each one refuses to face the world, even for a moment. Then, there are days when boredom, curiosity, want, need, rationality, and the right dose of confidence blend together in just the right way, and the front door opens enough for one or all of them to fit through if they turn sideways.

I monitor the changes from a distance, through brief phone calls, and text messages. Signs of improvement filter through casual conversations like the sun's rays filtering through the clouds.

"It took an hour to clean up the front yard."

"We've been working on Grant's car."

Though I am sure that they retreat to the house quickly enough, I zero in on these positive indicators. Each simple statement is an affirmation. With each affirmation, they seem a little less fragile. Strength isn't always a leap from here to there. Strength comes from all the small steps in between.

One day, Charlie ventures as far as the farmers market. He likes those peaches. Simple motivation. Positive reinforcement in the form of a juicy peach. Nothing eventful happens on his journey to or from the market. Though only a couple of blocks, as he makes his way down the cracked and worn sidewalks, he passes parked cars, children, dogs, sprinklers, and bicycles. He tolerates traffic, noise, and light to get there. A simple task that others would take for granted; for him, it is a sweet success—as sweet as the peach itself.

As legal matters go, the boys are given an additional thirty days to vacate. January 31st is now the final date, though the extra month does little to ease my tension. My dreams are now riddled with diving boards and plank walks. Jumping without a parachute becomes a recurring theme. I manage to project a positive attitude in my waking hours.

Soon, the boys are driving to farther destinations. With the Mustang still out of commission, the old Jeep is as much a communal property as the dog. Nia, always up for an adventure, takes to napping by the now revolving front door, ready and waiting for the next person that needs her accompaniment.

Charlie enjoys frequent walks through the neighborhood with her, though he prefers to walk mostly at night. I assume this is military-related, although I don't ask. It has been a year and nine months. These are forward steps.

Slowly but surely, their worlds expand as they seek out other places suitable for their companion. At first, they venture only to other dog parks; but soon, they realize there are trails, parks, and forests waiting to be explored in the crisp September air.

Nia provides not only opportunities for exploring the outdoors, but for socializing too. Well, sort of. She is quite good at it in her own way, crashing into runners and walkers alike on the wooded trails around Austin. Though the boys steer her clear of small children and bicycle riders, there are inevitable collisions. They are finally experiencing glimpses of Austin with Nia by their side, running along happily with a tree branch in her mouth.

Nia now sports her own backpack when she is out, one of the packages I have sent, and a direct result of having checked the mailbox. A simple piece of canvas slung over her back with nylon bands, one crossing her chest, the other buckled under her belly. The deep pockets on both sides allow her to carry her own water and hold the boy's necessities, mostly cell phones, and sunglasses.

Nia is a conversation starter. When the boys are out, people inevitably approach to pet her and ask questions.

"Is that a red Doberman?"

"Is she a purebred?"

"How old is she?"

The boys' first reaction to these inquiries is avoidance. They are only there for the dog and will endure the presence of others just enough to expose her to new surroundings. Curious people and too much stimulation soon force them back to the protective confines of the house.

Interestingly, James has succeeded in teaching Nia to step between them and oncoming strangers. With a subtle cue from him and a quick maneuver of her body, Nia serves as a barrier, enabling the boys to keep a comfortable distance. This is easy for her, the dog that craves human contact. Her happiest place, even in the midst of the ever-enticing outdoors, is close to the men she loves and protects. She remains near until she receives the command to release. She'll often hesitate, as though assessing the situation before distancing herself and continuing on with her enthusiastic enjoyment of the park.

Nia's manners have become impeccably precise as she learns to stay close by their sides when walking, to stop and sit before crossing streets, and to wait patiently for the command before proceeding. While James does most of the training, Grant and Charlie reinforce it, and all three benefit from an ever-increasing list of voice commands and hand signals.

With time, they slowly perfect the art of mumbling a few words to the strangers who want to know more about their dog. It's as much conversation as they will tolerate for a while, but they are making an effort.

Back home, courtesy of James' ever-developing dog training skills, Nia has acquired an even more extensive bag of tricks. She can give a high five and lie down on command. She stays, crawls, picks up, and drop items on request, and retrieves specific things from around the house. Always an expert at opening doors, she can now close them behind her. She has been trained to "sweep the house" upon their return, going through the front door ahead of them with a gesture. She rushes through each room, inspecting the areas for intruders—once proudly returning with a mouse in her jaws. The safety measure seems unnecessary as no outsider ever enters the house except me. *Oh well.* There are aspects of PTSD that I will never relate to.

As pleased as I am with the improvements, there are setbacks, days when no one will move. Matters of the mind cannot be forced. Still, they are getting better—and intriguing to me—all three are doing it at the same time. Then again, they are extraordinarily close and have weathered the same situations, and they are all on the same medication—daily doses of Nia.

36

IMPROVEMENT

CHARLIE RELATES that he has removed the soft top of the
Wrangler. His intent is only to replace the shredded, leaky
canvas before the weather turns, but I read this as a sure sign
that he is getting better. Until a replacement can be located,
he is no longer securely enclosed. Now, each time Nia steps
out the front door, she takes an immediate left toward the
driveway and effortlessly jumps into the back of the vehicle.
Unable to differentiate between leaving the house for a walk
or for a car ride, she does this almost every time until she
notices that her companion is walking down the street. Then
she hops out, lands on the driveway, and quickly catches up.
There is no need to coach her from the vehicle. The boys
know that Nia will stay near, as she always does.

Having spent one crisp fall afternoon hiking at a nearby
park with the dog, James and Grant are ready to head home.
Crossing the parking lot, they sprint to the Jeep. Nia sprints
behind them and, as usual, bounds into the back of the
Wrangler. Unfortunately, it is the Wrangler parked next to

them. This one, as it happens, has a driver in the front seat as well, and he drives forward at the same time as James, unaware that he has a stowaway. James heads out of the parking lot, not realizing that anything is amiss. Grant focuses on finding a good radio station. As they turn onto the main road, the Wrangler sputters and coughs while slowly gaining momentum. The other Jeep passes in the next lane. A happy Nia sits upright in the back seat.

Glancing over to admire the Jeep, Grant notices that the dog in the back looks almost exactly like theirs... Flashing lights, yelling, waving of arms and much horn honking ensue until the transfer can be made.

As Charlie relays the incident over the phone, Sarah and I dissolve into tears of laughter. Though I know that panic must have set in, I will wish forever after that I could have seen James and Grant when they realized that Nia was riding down the road in front of them. Charlie feigns anger at the others for almost losing the dog, but I note a slight chuckle in his voice. It is good to hear him lighten up.

"It could have happened to anyone," I remind him, laughing so hard I can barely get the words out.

37

GOOD THERAPY

COUNSELING CONTINUES FOR ME. I find it surprising how committed I am. I've never been a very dedicated person unless there is cake involved. After work, each Tuesday while Sarah attends her dance class, I walk next door to the counseling center. The dance studio and my new therapist's office are in the same strip mall. Aside from the car, my alternative is to sit in the studio's crowded lobby with the other moms. Therapy is easily the lesser evil.

The waiting room is stark. A former real estate office, it has individual rooms that are actually small movable cubicles. There are no other clients on Tuesday evenings. The therapist locks the front door behind me. An unusual setting perhaps, but I have seen worse, and I like her. I feel comfortable talking to her about my issues, and she listens actively, pointing out positive notes where I hadn't even seen them.

We cover a lot. It only lasts an hour—one session, one hour, once a week—but it's an hour of personal growth, of collecting my thoughts, reflecting on the past week, or month or year. She doesn't just listen—she hears and skillfully guides. It helps. The work is mine to do, and it is work, hard work. I feel sorry for myself. I rail against myself. I lose my way. I find it again. Some days I note remarkable headway. Some days I wonder why I'm there at all. Then I remember the lobby of the dance studio, and I keep going.

"It's like this," I try my best to explain one rainy Tuesday evening. "When I fill out those forms in the doctor's office, the ones that ask for *prior medical history*, I check things off that understandably raise concerns—cancer, check; pulmonary embolism, check; endocarditis, check." With each check, I slash my finger through the air for emphasis.

"Like checking yes to *criminal record* on a job application, eyebrows start raising, heads nod. Suddenly, I need more tests and scans than the average person. I need a consult with oncology and another with a cardiologist, then pulmonary. My chart has red flags all over it. No stone is left unturned. *Everything* is scrutinized." I sigh. "The general consensus is that my current symptoms may be much more serious than they appear, and *that* makes me worry."

"You don't want to give your full medical history," she states, echoing my thoughts.

"I know it's important, but if I didn't check those boxes, I would just be a patient like any other patient, a blank slate, nothing much here to worry about.

She rests her chin in her hand and speaks almost wistfully. "I would prefer not to have to answer yes to some of those questions myself. But I want my doctor to have all the information he needs to do his job."

"The doctor is being thorough," I acknowledge. "And I'm being accurate. It's my responsibility as a patient. It's counterproductive, I know, but if I didn't offer my *entire* medical history, a doctor might be inclined to say to me, *Oh, stop worrying! It's probably nothing!* And then... I would."

I look up at the gray ceiling, imagining the moment of serenity. A bubble-shaped skylight is dotted with raindrops that trickle slowly to the edges.

"Would you?" she asks gently.

Her question floats in the air. I don't answer. I shift my gaze from ceiling to floor. It's in that silence that I accept things for what they are, if only for the moment.

38

RELIEF

THEIR NEW-FOUND exposure to the outside world brings fresh challenges and forces the boys to deal with feelings that they have suppressed in their self-induced isolation. Having long since perfected the art of S.N.A.P., as I only half-jokingly coin their Serious Need to Avoid People, Charlie is forced into confrontation one day at a park. It isn't the dog park where he finds himself on this late October afternoon. He has arrived at a popular place for runners and bike riders. There, on the outskirts of Austin, well-worn trails twist through miles of woods offering a cool respite from the Indian summer sun. The parking lot contains an assortment of SUVs and trucks outfitted for the outdoors. Cars sport bike and roof racks, cargo carriers and the occasional canoe, affirming the enormous popularity of Austin's open spaces.

As Charlie tells it, he has knelt to adjust his running shoe in the lot while Nia drifts away, curiosity luring her to the opposite end of the Jeep. As she inspects new smells on the asphalt, a lone passerby, an older man, fifties maybe, dressed in bike shorts and helmet, approaches.

From Charlie's location at the front of the Jeep, he hears the distinct sound of a click and then, "It's okay. I've got you."

Charlie rises and steps around to the back.

"Hey," he says, surprised by the scene he finds at the rear of his vehicle.

The man stands in the parking lot, a neon leash in his hand. Nia is attached to the other end.

"This dog should be on a leash," he says, glaring at Charlie.

"Not your leash," Charlie answers.

"I thought he was a stray."

"There's a collar on that dog," Charlie speaks slowly, deliberately, so there won't be any misunderstanding. "And I'm standing right here."

As Charlie details the incident, I imagine the scene, the heat rising to his face, his eyes narrowing as a familiar wave of anger rushes over him.

Who does this guy think he is? This is Nia at the end of the lead. This is *his* dog, his prized possession, an animal he would die for. What does this stranger think he is doing? Does this man actually intend to walk away with the dog?

The man makes no effort to release the dog. He is only a few feet from Charlie. It crosses Charlie's mind that he can easily break his neck.

His voice menacingly low now, Charlie speaks again. "Let go of the dog."

Seconds, that's all the time this guy's got. One move in the wrong direction and Charlie will be on him. *It will be nothing. One more violent scene.* It will feel good to release the anger that has surfaced so suddenly inside him.

Charlie places his cell phone on the ground. He stands ready. All he needs is one signal, one excuse, one second...

Alarmed by Charlie's stance and the icy look in his eyes, the man unhooks the lead and, without a word, backs away from Charlie and the dog. Having backed a sufficient distance, he quickly turns and leaves.

Taking a step back, unable to breathe, Charlie circles around to the side of his vehicle and pulls himself onto the passenger seat, shaken by the intensity of his own feelings, surprised that he has been so out of control.

Had he really just decided to kill that man? He tries to focus on the fact that it is Nia. It would have been justified. If it had been some inanimate object, it would have been different, right? If someone had been trying to steal his Jeep, would it have been different? The very thought makes him angry. He tries to get control, but his mind is racing.

Had he really been ready to kill some stupid guy? In a park? In Texas? This isn't Iraq. He isn't in a war. How can it come so easily to him?

Thoughts of what he should have done, what other, *normal* people would have done, crowd his mind. This is not something he can talk out in some therapy session. Just how would that go? I want to kill people. Seriously, I may do it.

Maybe he shouldn't go out. Maybe he isn't fit to live among society when the thought of killing can come over him just like that...

Alarmed at his retelling of the event, I try to interject.

Changing the subject has long been my chosen strategy to help him regain composure, but Charlie continues.

A passerby interrupts his thoughts. "Everything okay, man?"

Charlie realizes he has been sitting with his head in his hands. Nia has perched in the driver seat appearing poised and composed in comparison.

"Marines, huh?" The stranger nods toward a sticker on the Jeep windshield. "Me, too." He pauses. "It's tough," he says almost to himself as he walks away. "It's tough to come home too."

The stranger begins to jog as he enters a trail leading into the woods. Charlie sits, stroking Nia's head. His mind picks up where it left off. Trying to erase the thoughts, he feels a sudden urgency to run. Charlie exits his Jeep and heads towards the trail, the dog bounding after him. In his mind, he keeps replaying everything, struggling to make sense of it all. He is soon deep into the cool, dark woods. Trees blur as he speeds down the trail, not aware of his direction, trying to outrun his thoughts. He flies across dry creek beds, over logs, up rocky inclines. Nia, agile as a cat, keeps up easily.

Why can't I control this? How can I stop the rage? What is wrong with me? His breathing labored, his eyes wet, Charlie plays back in his mind all he has experienced, the violence he has witnessed. It seems so surreal—like he has been in another world, a world where different rules apply and one can be sure of nothing.

Keep running, he tells himself, though his legs are numb. You're home now. You can't go around killing people. You're not there anymore.

Off the trail now, Charlie runs faster and faster, breaking tree limbs as he crashes through the thickening forest, tearing skin and clothing. Blood, now oozing from his arms, offers a strange sense of release. When his legs can no longer move, and his breathing is too labored to continue, he collapses to the ground. Deep in the forest, lying on his back, chest pounding, he looks up through blurred eyes at the treetops and the sky beyond. The sun glistens down through the trees in long rays of light, beckoning him to grab hold and pull himself up. He lays there, arms out to his sides. He couldn't move them if he were drowning, dead weights that they are.

Has he outrun it? Has he run so far and so fast from the thoughts that haunt him that he has lost them? He isn't angry anymore. Exhausted and bleeding, with aching sides and throbbing legs, he no longer fights the thoughts in his head.

Nia lies on the ground next to him, her tongue hanging to one side, her gums bright red as she struggles to catch her breath. She tries to rest her head on his heaving chest. Suddenly aware of her presence, Charlie looks down at her. Her head bounces up and down as his chest rises and drops. Her eyes are glazed over, white foam drips from her mouth. Covered in burrs, dirt, and sticks, she resembles some crazed lunatic. She is such a startling sight that Charlie suddenly laughs.

"Owwww."

His sides convulse in pain, and yet he can't suppress it. He laughs uncontrollably as he watches the deranged animal on top of him bob up and down on his chest, and there, somewhere in his laughter, his last drop of emotion is extinguished.

The two of them lay there for a long while—their breathing less labored—the quiet calm of the woods now palpable. A soft breeze gently rustles the brown leaves overhead, and they fall to the ground around him. Charlie rises slowly and painfully, brushing off dirt, smearing blood. With his still crazed-looking companion by his side, he tries to find his way back to the trail.

Filthy, exhausted, and very possibly lost, Charlie feels better than he has in a long time. His head is clear. He has dealt with the growing rage inside of him, and he has regained control. He can breathe. It isn't a permanent fix, he knows, but pain and anger have subsided for now, and it feels good.

That's how it's going to happen, he decides on his long walk back. A little at a time, but it can happen. He will do whatever is necessary to fight it until he wins. He has won this time. He will win again. Charlie recognizes not only that he has a sickness but also has a cure. For the first time, he feels in control of his anger and hopeful. It is a long way back, generously long in its restoring benefits. Up ahead, finally, he sees a light that is the edge of the woods, and the two of them head out.

39

POSSIBILITIES

I SUGGEST appointments with the VA for Grant and James, but they show no interest in following through. The very thought of the VA screams *disability* to them. Some of our returning military will never pass through those doors, and while it has many benefits, I know that it is not the only way, and not necessarily the best way to get the help they need. The VA is not without its glaring faults. It can involve mountains of paperwork, agonizingly long waits, and help that will not come soon enough for some. Support can be found elsewhere through a physician, a private therapist, a religious organization, or a supportive family. One has only to reach out or stay connected.

Grant is doing much better and is in close contact with his family. Charlie has kept an open mind and, with some prodding, has taken those important first steps toward professional help. James remains, for the most part, secluded in the house, not interested or capable of accessing these options. Apart from brief escapes to parks and trails, his transition is painfully, almost hopelessly nonexistent, except for one thing.

Charlie mentions that James had returned to Zoom Room for Nia's Good Citizen test. They hadn't needed classes or additional training. Nia passed the test easily and quickly. No challenge there. Not long after, James emails me a copy of the signed certificate. Working with the dog is clearly a key to James' recovery. There has to be a way to use it. I focus on possibilities.

Each of the boys had paid into the Post-9/11 Montgomery G.I. Bill during their enlistment, and they are eligible to use it for school and technical training. Armed with this knowledge, I hunt online for schools that teach people to be professional dog trainers. I narrow my search to only those that clearly state the GI Bill is accepted as a payment option.

Lots of schools across the country offer training. I zero in on one state-approved school in Texas, just outside of Austin. Offering "certification in the science of dog training," it includes basic to advanced obedience, personal protection, police K-9 training, assisted therapy, scent detection, behavior modification, and much more. Class sessions are four, eight, and twelve weeks. The schedule of classes, lectures, and field training looks a little daunting.

Would James be up for the challenge?

I print out the twenty-page brochure and, during my lunch break from work, drop it at the post office, having addressed the package to James with a note inquiring whether he would be interested.

In about a week, I receive a text message. It simply says, "Yes."

A crack in the armor.

The school requires a completed application, an essay denoting why one would choose to attend their academy, a deposit, and two recommendations. Classes are attended on a full-time basis. One major plus, it includes on-site housing. Upon acceptance, students can begin at the start of the next session, January 14th, the same month the house will be gone.

That evening after work, I hurriedly call the school, grateful for the one-hour time difference that means they will be open. The head of admissions happily offers more information about the school. Many dogs, she tells me, are selected from animal shelters and trained in basic obedience, giving the students a chance to work with different animals and making the dogs more desirable for adoption. They have a marvelous success record for the dogs—converting unsocialized, timid, even aggressive animals into well-behaved family pets. It's a win-win situation for prospective trainers, the dogs they handle, and the future owners of those dogs. Selected dogs that show promise can go on to more intense training, becoming valuable search and rescue dogs, therapy dogs, guide dogs, and more. It is not uncommon for students to adopt the dogs, having developed strong bonds during their intense training.

In addition to being a school for future professionals, it is also a boarding facility and offers training for personally owned dogs. To my one-track mind, this spells future employment for James.

Facilities include an event center, a swimming pool for

dogs only, an obstacle course, and indoor/outdoor climate-controlled kennels. Student housing consists of shared mobile homes on the 350-acre property. The school offers career counseling and job placement assistance. I already know that the Montgomery G.I. Bill will cover the entire program, including the housing stipend and textbooks. The director assures me that this is possible.

"In fact," she adds, "we have a student who is currently attending the academy courtesy of the G.I. bill."

The application will require two recommendations, among other things. She reiterates the importance of this.

"The program isn't for everyone," she explains, her voice suddenly serious. "It takes an extraordinary amount of commitment. Those that make it through the entire program are the most dedicated. There are starter courses, refresher classes, certainly shorter programs, but those individuals that complete the entire program are at the top of their craft, and they are in demand. It is those few quality trainers that I specialize in presenting to the world."

Her passionate speech hooks me. But this is about James, not me. James is a marine. He possesses the level of training and ability that she is hinting at, and James is a master at training Nia. This can be a successful endeavor—if we can only get him out of the house.

40

RECOMMENDATIONS

I IMMEDIATELY SIT down to write James' first written recommendation. I seek the help of Michelle at Zoom Room for the second one. A professional dog trainer herself, she can vouch for having observed James working with Nia. She will be a perfect recommendation for him if she will consider it.

She will not, however, feel comfortable providing the recommendation. She explains her reasoning, mentioning that she is familiar with the academy and with their sometimes negative training techniques of which she does not approve. In addition, she had encouraged James to bring in Nia regularly, but he made no further effort after passing the CGC. She could be persuaded to change her mind if he would continue the work.

"I understand. Thank you," I respond.

I do understand her point of view. If she only knew how big a step it was for him to have visited her facility at all, how this is his sole motivation to leave the house, and the one possibility of reconnecting him with the world. Negative training techniques are a smaller consideration to me right now. My focus is on motivating a veteran who is suffering from extended PTSD. He will make his own choices about which techniques are useful when presented with them all. His deep connection with Nia will not allow him to mistreat her, no matter what the training. His patience and understanding will help him to perfect his craft. This is an important opportunity for him. Even more important, he is willing to try.

Frustrated, I open my laptop and write a second letter of recommendation for James. I change the wording. I focus on different abilities. Somewhat desperate now, I even write his required essay stating why he wishes to attend this particular school. Upon receiving it via email, he indicates he will write his own.

Fine, I laugh to myself. Self-motivation is the operative word here, but I didn't think my essay was that bad.

In the coming week, James obtains a second recommendation, although I will never know where or how he gets it. He requests his high school transcript and military record. He fills out the application and, amazingly, borrows the Jeep and hand-delivers everything to the school. While there, he tours the facilities with other prospective students, getting his first look at the place. Having submitted all the required paperwork; there is nothing left to do but wait. Time is short, very short.

41

EXPENSES

I SIFT through a pile of credit card bills that have been steadily racking up with airline tickets and expenses, mostly to Austin. I feel guilty leaving Sarah with family and friends, although she enjoys the freedom. At fifteen, she seems to have thrived on her independent childhood. I question whether I am really helping Charlie at all.

"It would be cheaper to just move there," I say softly, sitting on my bed sorting and stacking envelopes.

"We can't move. We live here," Sarah warns over her shoulder.

She has been helping herself to my closet, holding up various pieces of clothing in front of the mirror.

"You can help him from here," she says, as though reading my mind. Sifting through my clothing, she appears much older than her years. She's grown. I hadn't noticed lately.

"Maybe." I sigh. "Maybe he doesn't need my help."

"Oh, yes, he does!" She models a blue dress, which looks much better on her petite figure than it ever did on mine.

"I don't know," I hesitate. "He doesn't ask for it."

"People ask in different ways."

"Thanks, my wise little Buddha-child," I tell her, but she has already vacated the room with my favorite heels.

I glance at the calendar above my desk. The date to relinquish their house looms in a big red circle, and they still have no plan. Ten weeks to go.

Leave them alone. Fear of being homeless is a good motivator. They are smart. Surely they will seek out a solution.

And what if they don't? What will their future hold? What a shame that these young veterans might have to move back in with family, having been unable to transition on their own. I had suggested that exact scenario to Charlie several times.

"Come home for a while," I had implored him. "Re-group."

Charlie met my suggestion with immediate resistance. This was not his desired direction. More than that, home for Charlie was a memory of my parenting flaws, although he didn't say so. Besides, his home was no longer there. I had moved to Florida during his enlistment. He didn't see the farmhouse as his home. Okay, then. I understood. But moving forward is such a painstakingly slow process for them, and soon, circumstance will take over, whether they are ready or not. Unwilling to stay with family and lacking other plans, they may find that the next step is a shelter.

Certainly, dogs aren't allowed at homeless shelters. I

maintain hope that they will refuse to part with Nia, that they will want to provide *her* with a home, even if they don't care about themselves. They will surely take care of her, and in doing so, they will take care of themselves.

Preparing for the worst, just the same, I research the cost to fly a seventy-six-pound dog to Florida.

42

GETTING BETTER

THERAPY SEEMS to be helping me, along with anti-anxiety medication. I have tried medications in the past. Now I give them time to work. Patience. It's an important key to my recovery. I tell myself that my panic attacks always subside if I can just wait them out.

The passage of time is of equal importance. It has been years since my original health scares, years of panic, worry, and tests. I'm still here, still okay, still alive.

In addition, even with my extensive research into the world of communicable diseases, I have failed to convince medical experts that I display the classic symptoms of MRSA, Lyme Disease, West Nile Virus, dengue fever, Ebola, or rabies. And I am still alive.

I am still alive.

I continue my regular therapy appointments. I listen as the therapist tells me the same thing, week after week. Slowly, very slowly, I accept that maybe, just maybe, it could be true.

I meditate. I try to get more sleep. I walk during my lunch breaks—it's calming. Baby steps, yes, but I'm not saving the world here, I'm just trying to get out of my own way. I tell myself that I am not dying, not today, not right now. As my body relaxes, my physical symptoms begin to subside.

Coincidentally, my computer breaks, and I temporarily lose my phone. I can no longer look up symptoms or diagnosis. Though panicked at first, I soon realize this is oddly freeing. Stomachaches, headaches, weird aches and pains, and strange illnesses happen less. Sanity begets health. Health begets sanity. A simple concept, easily obtainable to some, achieved only through continuous, diligent effort for me.

I have setbacks, occasionally visiting the ER, clutching my fabricated symptoms like some noxious security blanket—afraid to touch it, afraid to let it go. Only sporadically now do I subject myself to disapproving glances as I try to convince medical personnel that my symptoms are life-threatening.

My attacks come on when I am under stress from life events that feel out of my control. As a result, I focus internally, and that focus leads to panic. Recognition, a huge step in my progress, takes countless hours of treatment to achieve but gives me control over my thoughts. I know what I am doing and why I'm doing it. Now I have the tools to stop it.

I wish that I could say I hiked the Appalachian Trail in some soul-searching expedition, culminating in a moment of self-realization, or that I had journeyed to some exotic locale in search of inner peace. I did none of that. My successes come from short intervals of work in a therapist's office, pounding my head against reality, and then only obtained in increments. There is no bright, shining moment of clarity, the kind where you get to stand on top of the mountain and shout, "I did it." Mine is a continuous fight within me, against me. It's tough psychological work. Being normal does not come easy to me.

And, as much as I believe in the importance of animals as therapy, I made my journey without a dog by my side. She is busy helping other people. So am I. That, too, has been a key to getting better. Helping the boys allows me to experience moments when I am confident.

As the therapist interjects during one session, "We try so hard not to die, sometimes we forget to live."

I recognize, slowly but surely, that my focus is shifting.

43

A BREAK

One November morning, as I sit down at my desk at work, I receive a text message from James.

"Getting nervous," he types. "Haven't heard anything about that school. Maybe I didn't get in."

I sigh. Classes would have begun for him soon. I glance at the calendar. Only six weeks away. There will be no more extensions on the house. With student housing, it would have been a two-fold blessing—more time to find another place to live and valuable career training.

I try to focus on other schools I had researched. Hadn't there been one in Oregon or maybe it was Colorado? Defeated, I slump back in my chair. There is so little time to pursue other schools. Without therapy, counseling, or medication, James continues to simply exist in the house—and soon that will no longer be an option.

A second text comes an hour later.

"Got in. Just got an email. Start next week."

"Oh, thank God." I don't care if the whole office hears.

Students bring their own dogs with them to the school. The boys agree that James will take Nia. All three boys accompany the dog to a vet, where she receives the required physical exam, heartworm and fecal tests and vaccines, her first appointment since her arrival in Austin.

Don't put all your eggs in one basket. Have a back-up plan. Be open to other options. All good advice yes, but if your ship is slowly sinking and only one lifeline exists, one had better grab on with everything you have. I can only hope that James will hold tight to the rope and pull himself up.

44

LIGHT

I HAD RECONCILED myself to the fact that Charlie would stay with us in Florida whether he liked it or not. No son of mine will be out on the street. His pride and ego be damned —with no plan of his own, there is no more time for patience.

Then, a breakthrough—Charlie hesitantly reports that medication seems to be helping. He feels more in control of his anger, he tells me. He has begun jogging daily, and the exercise helps him as well.

I ask how he would feel about returning to school. Expecting negativity, I continue anyway, illustrating how he qualifies for benefits under the G.I. Bill and would get a housing stipend and money to cover his books. I suggest a nearby community college. Charlie indicates he will think about it.

It's a vague response, but I take it as a positive one. We have been here once before, many years ago. It's all I have. I run with it.

We've got to move fast. Classes begin shortly after the

Christmas break. He needs to apply for his benefits quickly and obtain his high school transcripts. A Declaration of Eligibility from the VA will follow.

I will myself to slow down. One day at a time, one step at a time, sometimes one minute at a time—the problem is we are running out of time.

I barely remember Christmas this year. Charlie stays in Texas. Sarah and I stay home. Preoccupied, we've made no plans, and I can't afford the travel expenses anyway.

A visit to the therapist secures an added prescription for Charlie, to ease anxiety if he needs it. He navigates his way through the blur of admissions, class choices, schedules, and campuses. Sarah and I assist from Florida, going over times and locations of the classes. We come up with a workable schedule, only to discover that a class is full or canceled, causing a domino effect and forcing us to change the schedule again.

We scour Craigslist for housing, and in a stroke of luck, stumble across a military veteran renting a room near campus. Charlie agrees to meet with him. Arrangements are made. With no credit or employment check and a reasonable deposit, the official move-in date is the first of January. The owner even throws in a mattress. The stars have aligned again. Charlie has a place to lay his head.

Sarah emails the winning schedule to Charlie for his approval, calls me at work to head off further changes, tracks down most of the textbooks at discounted rates, submits the information to the school and to the G.I. Bill representative, and ultimately saves Charlie from succumbing to the anxiety that has threatened to derail his college aspirations altogether.

Even without the constant friction between us, school for Charlie had never come easily. It wasn't that he didn't try. He was simply unable to focus. Typical of those diagnosed with attention deficit disorder, he had trouble concentrating, was easily bored and lacked self-motivation.

Some of these learning difficulties have improved, and his military training has fostered self-discipline, but he faces college with additional challenges. Depression, anxiety, and a strong desire for avoidance now top the list. I let out a slow breath. It will be a miracle if he shows up for school, much less does well. I try to imagine James or Grant going with him, or just hanging out by the Jeep, awaiting his return from class. I brush the thought aside. I know this won't happen. Close though they may be, they are not babysitters. Charlie will have to do this alone.

He does. Charlie works his way through his first class, then his second. Somehow, he keeps up with the coursework, pulls it all together, and presents himself each day. Grateful to have gotten the classes he wants given the short notice—he works diligently. The syllabus is not the problem.

Sitting in the back of the room, he refuses to participate. The hood of his sweatshirt strategically placed over his head almost covers his eyes, perspiration drips down his temples, and his hands sink into his pockets. This becomes his typical routine, quiet observer, glancing at the clock until relief comes, and they all stand to leave. He makes every effort to bypass the instructor, carefully avoiding eye contact as he exits the room, rushing back to the safety of his vehicle, then the house.

Charlie mentions that he feels much older than most

students, although he is the same age or just slightly older. He doesn't dislike his classmates; he just feels *different*. The sterile learning environment seems so far removed from his experiences. The countries they discuss are places he has lived. The politics of war, he has witnessed firsthand. Charlie feels a profound disconnect, having seen and experienced so much more than most of these students will ever know.

Other servicemen attend classes too. He can easily spot them. They are guarded, sometimes jumpy, sometimes uncomfortable when the class gets loud. They don't interact the same.

I understand his difficulties, and I'm proud of him for sticking with the plan.

"You're doing it," I remind him constantly, as though I am afraid he may forget.

45

DESPERATE MEASURES

WHILE CHARLIE SURVIVES his first few days of classes, James doesn't. Paralyzed by anxiety, James skips his first day at the academy and remains in his room the entire day. The others joke that he may have peed in there, or worse. I can only imagine what it takes to try again the next day, but try he does.

Charlie drops off James and Nia at the school on day two, assuming a lack of transportation will force him to stay. Using ingenuity to find a ride, James reappears at the house with Nia that evening.

"He's not leaving," Charlie relays in a phone call the next morning. "I can't force him into the Jeep. He's supposed to live there, isn't he? I have class. I can't drive him every day, even if he would get in the car."

"Just go," I tell him.

Charlie has his own challenges. His focus on moving forward right now is as brittle as glass. The slightest tap has the potential to shatter his efforts. Dismayed, I drive to work while telepathically willing James to go to school. *You can do it. You really want to do this. Just please try...*

I will never know the thought process that drove him. He was at a critical crossroads. The next morning, alone in a house that is all but gone, James somehow must decide in which direction he wants his life to go. If professional dog training is his choice, he will have to move mountains to get there.

Charlie and Grant return to the house that evening just as the police knock on the door. It would seem, the officers tell the boys, that the neighbor's car has been stolen. Have they noticed anything suspicious?

Inexplicably, the car reappears undamaged later that evening, parked down the street. James squeezes in the front door with no comment. No charges are ever filed. Charlie drives James and Nia back to the academy the same evening, where this time James stays. Day three is a success.

Sometimes the best we can hope for is to learn from our mistakes. Failing that, just scraping by without legal consequences can be good enough.

At the academy, Nia proves herself a valuable assistant to James. The long hours spent working together assimilate them easily. Even among so many other dogs, Nia remains centered on him. James stays focused on Nia too, in an effort to block out the stress. Out of his safe zone, he has nowhere to hide. Having refused professional counseling and anti-anxiety medications, he has no support except for the dog. I hold my breath.

46

MOVING ON

GRANT MOVES on to share an apartment with his brother, though he remains in touch. He seems to have pulled ahead of the others more easily. Generally a happy-go-lucky sort of guy, he has a different psychological makeup. His mother and his younger sister are now within driving distance, and he visits them regularly. He, too, had a rough transition back to civilian life, but his self-imposed isolation seems to have allowed him to process all that he has been through. The emotional downtime benefited him on his road to recovery, reinforcing my belief in mandatory decompression periods.

Had he landed full-throttle into the world of family responsibilities, jobs, bills, the pressures of everyday life, I fear he may not have fared as well. For Grant, the time spent in the Austin house was an important step in his re-acclimation. The danger is in allowing that recovery period to stagnate, to not use it as a time to heal. When one is in a prolonged, psychologically anesthetized state, meaningful employment wanes, relationships fall away, and problems compound.

During my visits, Grant had moments when he was quiet, introspective. At times, he didn't join in the conversation as readily, and I knew there was more under the surface. It relieves me that Grant has moved on successfully and yet, like a wounded animal that heals in captivity and is released back into the wild, his departure stirs a mixture of joy and sadness in my heart.

47

SETBACKS

S̲ETBACKS ARE an inevitable part of the healing process. Therapy for Charlie comes to an uncomfortable standstill when the VA psychologist asks him, "What is it going to take to get you to stop coming here?"

Perhaps these aren't the exact words used, but this is what Charlie hears. He relays the statement to me over the phone that evening.

"He probably meant, what can I do to help you more, to feel like maybe you didn't need therapy anymore," I suggest, but Charlie refuses to see the therapist again.

"Maybe a different therapist..." I venture.

From my own experience, I know that some therapists don't fit. Charlie had been progressing. Having a professional to talk with was helping him. Finding a new therapist is wishful thinking. There is no other therapist available at the VA—even if Charlie was open to it.

The phone call leaves me angry. Part of me wants to confront a professional who would not choose his words more carefully. In a vulnerable position, what patient wouldn't react to any words that sound negative? For those veterans desperately searching to regain their sense of self, positive reinforcement plays a key role in getting there. Sadly, Charlie's hard work has been dashed by one ill-spoken sentence.

Does this man have any clue how he has been interpreted? Did Charlie, who had been doing so well, take a light statement as an excuse to sabotage his efforts? I resign myself to the fact that I will never know.

48

LOOKING FORWARD

I STOP SEEKING EMERGENCY ROOMS. My emergencies are
expensive and time-consuming. My counseling sessions are
expensive. I simply have to choose one or the other, I
reason.

Me. Reasoning.

In addition to my more discerning state of mind, by this
time I have undergone such a multitude of blood tests, scans,
MRIs, and X-rays that I could tell the doctors what they will
find. I harbor a benign spot on my right lung, a harmless cyst
on an ovary, a hemangioma in my liver. I will, without fail,
develop lymphedema if you stick a needle in my left arm. I
know what medications my body will refuse to tolerate and
the consequences of forcing it to do so.

In a nod to the value of Internet research, I am secure in
the knowledge that you could remove your stomach, your
spleen, one kidney, eighty percent of your intestines, and
seventy-five percent of your liver and still survive. On a
lighter note, I know that I have triumphed over cancer, that

my pituitary gland is capable of spontaneous recovery and that adequate sleep qualifies as a powerful medicine.

I allow the gas gauge of my vehicle to creep a little lower —a bold move should there be an emergency. I finish off the suspicious looking leftovers in the fridge with only one thought—I'm hungry. I stop searching the Internet. At work, I log on and calmly enter an amount to be invested into a 401K, my focus shifting from beneficiaries to benefits. One particularly stressful court case prompts chest pains and a trip to the hospital—for one of the attorneys, not for me.

Sarah, in her first year of high school, is contemplating college choices. She expresses an interest in studying psychology.

"You guys are nuts," she jokes. "You need me."

Slowly, the boys navigate their new territories with Nia pushing and prodding them each step of the way. James now lives at the training facility; Charlie is in his newly rented room. Nia spends weekdays at the facility with James and weekends with Charlie.

The house succumbs to foreclosure. What little furniture there is remains. The boys take only personal possessions and, of course, the grill. Not sure where it will go but reluctant to leave it behind, the three of them carry it around the side of the house and secure it to the Jeep with such great care that I question their emotional attachment to the steel.

The training dummy, loosely wrapped in carpet, which now imparts the illusion that he may have legs, is rolled out of the house only to be inexplicably abandoned in the front yard. Leaning against the pecan tree, he causes many a startled passerby to jump back in horror.

The next day the locks are changed. A notice on the door indicates that trespassers will be prosecuted. They have moved on just in time.

49

ACCESS

Like Charlie, James finds it difficult to integrate into his new surroundings. Nia remains at his side, easing the stress when it becomes unbearable. Her presence calms him. She, too, is learning and can be nervous sometimes in her new surroundings. James senses when she needs his reassurance and the tables turn as he encourages her.

Had Charlie been allowed to take Nia to classes with him, would his adjustment be easier? If Nia was allowed to quietly lie at Charlie's feet or under his desk during class, a "tuck" command for many therapy dogs, would his transition be smoother? At this point in Charlie's recovery, I truly feel that a trained therapy dog will be of far greater value to him than Nia. He is reintegrating into society and navigating real-life situations. His greatest challenge, until now, has been the dog park. College is different territory. Nia is not allowed.

It is common practice for dogs to assist children in the courtroom. I have witnessed the positive effects many times. Accompanying children into the courtroom and sitting with them at the witness stand during their testimonies, court facility dogs can calm even the most nervous witness. Studies have confirmed that animate touch (holding a dog's leash or petting the animal) often assists a young witness who may be frightened about testifying. For child witnesses, the positive effects are immediate and profound.

Charlie is a soldier, not a child. And yet for adults, animals can bring about similar effects, drawing out even the most isolated. Praising an animal can help a traumatized veteran overcome emotional numbness. Teaching a dog service commands develops a person's ability to communicate, to be assertive but not aggressive—a distinction some veterans struggle with after their service. Dogs can ease the hypervigilance common in vets with PTSD. Some veterans report they can finally sleep knowing that a naturally alert soul is watching. A dog's presence can boost endorphins, the body's natural pain killers, and suppress epinephrine, the stress hormone. The calming influence and quiet emotional support of a dog would probably have helped Charlie in his new surroundings.

Regardless, Nia is not far away, and she eagerly awaits his return. Charlie knows she is close. As he takes those important first steps out into the world again—that will have to be enough.

50

RELIEF

Slowly, James and Charlie regain their footing. Each day is one more day that they survive. A month passes, and they are still there, both in their respective schools, neither one giving up, each of them in their separate houses, showering, dressing, and showing up.

One evening I receive a "recruiting" email from the director of the dog training academy, a follow-up to our much earlier conversation.

Has your friend made any decisions yet? Is he still interested in attending the academy?

I provide her with James' full name and inquire whether he is still a student there. After all his effort, is it possible that James is no longer there? Has he left school? Had he ever really gone at all?

Crestfallen, I sink into my chair. We are out of time. I am, sadly, out of options. Apparently, so is James.

The response comes moments later.

"I hadn't realized we were talking about James. Yes, he is here. He is one of my best students!"

Charlie steadily works his way through his first semester. He decides to major in government, a fitting choice considering his military background. In phone conversations, he shares little about his classes but reports that he no longer has a need to sit with his back to a wall, nor does he feel compelled to "scan the perimeters" of the parking lot. I sigh at the thought of the challenges he's had to overcome, yet, with each successfully completed class, I detect a slight shift in his tone. I could swear it sounds like confidence. Through the thick Texas mesquite, they are beginning to see the horizon.

James occasionally texts me that Nia is doing well in agility. She thrives on the challenge of the course, with its jumps, tunnels, bridges, and poles. The faster the better, he tells me. At times, her feet seem to barely touch the ground.

Of course, I think. *She had plenty of practice dodging my horses and sprinting over my furniture.*

She is exceptional in obedience classes as well, remaining so focused on James during trials that nothing can distract her. Border collies are put to shame by her hyper-focus. For this, I take no credit. Nia had been far from obedient when she lived with Sarah and me. But she possesses a strong desire to please those she loves. James has channeled that desire into a meticulous machine, capable of performing the most precise movements with almost imperceptible commands. The instructors are impressed. James looks like a genius. Nia is just happy.

Not surprisingly, James has developed a passion for the

art of training dogs, and just as I had suspected, he is exceptionally good at it. He understands the subtle nuances of communicating through body language. He assesses each animal's attention span and abilities and adjusts his methods accordingly. At the academy, he hones his skills: the tone of his voice, eye contact, timing, and patience. Even the most errant dog responds positively, and for James, the more difficult the dog, the more welcome the challenge. He moves the dogs easily through obedience and agility classes and on to more complex training.

James hopes to apply for a job at the academy, although that is still a long way off. The facilities are top-notch, the staff professional, qualities that resonate with his training as a soldier. His interest is in search and rescue or military dogs, having experienced the value of such animals first-hand. Still angst-ridden when leaving the property, and without a driver's license or vehicle, he considers the school his new safe place. Lucky for him, it provides much more than the Austin house. Here, there are new learning experiences and challenges with each new day. As he works with other dogs to gain their trust and confidence, he begins to gain his own.

It doesn't come easily. He fights daily, sometimes excruciatingly, with internal struggles. Initially unable to sleep, replaying the day's events over in his mind each evening and hypervigilant in his new surroundings at night, James drags himself through his classes until, at last, he collapses onto his bed one night and sleeps, really sleeps. Three weeks into the program, with his body finally rested, and his head clear, he has his first really good day, an integral turning point. The routine of scheduled classes, the physical demands of the job, and the opportunity to wind down at the end of a long day regulate his body and mind.

He eventually connects with the other students as well. Not too difficult, considering they all live in the same place with the same interests and similar goals. Each student possesses one or two of their own dogs that serve as focal points and ice-breakers. The animals fill student housing as they are allowed to reside with their owners. Interactions come more easily as dogs and people mesh together in this somewhat controlled environment. Therapy, for James, is finally found in life at the academy.

What a great concept. I imagine a world where all dog people live together, and all dogs go to work with them each day.

51

SUNSHINE

I stop communicating with the boys after their initial jump into life. I don't try to contact them. I don't mail any packages. This is not exactly by choice. I can't. They are out of the house, all three of them, and much too busy to take my phone calls. My assistance has been replaced by more important things and, oddly enough, I am deliriously happy about it.

What they need now is time. They are getting used to their new routines. I am getting used to mine. Bills that have been piling up slowly begin to downsize. I sleep more soundly. I enjoy more activities with Sarah. I focus on the horses again. I begin to compete in horse shows, something I haven't done since I was a kid. Without my constant overwhelming anxiety, I have space in my head and time in my days to do other things.

In February, I schedule a routine doctor appointment, a prescription refill requirement. The doctor asks how I am doing.

"I feel fine," I tell her.

"Any *issues*?" she asks out of the corner of her mouth as she peruses the computer screen in the exam room. I know she is expecting my usual—an anxious stream of imagined symptoms delivered with growing panic.

"Yes, my hair," I reply.

"Your hair?"

"I need a trim, but I haven't had time. And my weight," I add, smoothing my skirt with my palms. "But I'm working on that."

The doctor leans back in her chair, smiling, and suddenly we are discussing ordinary, everyday, *non-medical* topics. I detect an undeniable hint of relief in her demeanor. I am quite satisfied with myself as well.

After my appointment, I head toward the elevator and back out into the Florida sun. A new shoe store has opened nearby. It will mean a slight detour before heading home, but I have the afternoon free.

In April, James graduates at the top of his class. Immediately upon graduation, the academy offers him a job. With James' busy schedule and new responsibilities, Nia moves in with Charlie.

James' hard work at the school, not to mention his incredibly hard internal work, has paid off. In addition to a steady paycheck, he will get staff housing and opportunities for more specialized training, including chances to attend seminars and exhibitions throughout the country. The possibilities that will emerge for him in a field that he loves will be endless and exciting.

Though quite pleased with his success, none of us are

surprised at this development. We could all see what James had been unable to envision. Perhaps from his new position at the top, he will have a much better view.

Charlie goes to James' graduation ceremony. He tells me that they attended an after-party at a nearby bar and enjoyed the evening, much to their own surprise. Though still cautious, they are no longer paralyzed with anxiety. Two-and-a-half years after their military service has ended, all three boys are back on track, and on their way toward realizing their potential.

It will be years before they will consider applying for compensation from the military, even longer before they will talk about their military experiences, but they are now transitioning successfully. Each huge and difficult step gives them the ability to take on another and another, gaining a little more confidence and strength each time.

52

PICTURE

In April, I sit down at my computer and notice an email from James. The subject line reads "my business card." I draw a breath as my finger hits the keyboard to open it. There on the screen before me is the most beautiful picture of Nia, head slightly tilted, deep brown eyes peering inquisitively at the camera. It could have been a magazine cover. Underneath the photo is James' full name, and underneath that, "Animal Behavior Specialist."

Smiling, I gaze at the picture. We have all worked so hard to get here: the boys, me, even the dog. Especially the dog. I had sent Nia to Texas on a mission, and she worked relentlessly to rouse these boys from despondency and start them on paths to their futures. She pushed past their barriers and gently lured them out into the world, standing by their sides, supporting each of them as they went.

She had been my accomplice on this mission and my replacement when I couldn't be there. Nia possesses the heart of a soldier, the focus of a fox, and the patience of a saint. No clinical therapy or medication could have helped them the way she had.

The picture on the little business card is a beautiful testament to a story that isn't over, but that is continuing to get better every day.

53

MOMENTS

Years later, in a rare moment of reflection, Charlie will comment, "I was a wreck, Mom, a complete and total mess. I thought... maybe it would... I don't even know..."

On the other end of the phone, I cringe at the words. A part of me instinctively wants to cover my ears. It is what I had feared most, what I had almost refused to acknowledge. At the time, I hadn't known we were walking so close to the edge. To hear him articulate the thought, I'm instantly ashamed of my ignorance. Composing myself, I take a deep breath.

"Actually," I interrupt him, "I didn't know you were that strong."

Silence.

"Yeah," he says as if trying on the words for size. "Yeah," he repeats, adjusting the fit.

We talk for a while, a long while. We talk like two people who understand each other. I have helped him, he says. He has helped me, I tell him. We have a connection, now, far beyond what I could have ever hoped. We have walked this long road together though I may not have fully realized the significance at times. No regrets. I did what I could with what I had. I was there for him in my own off-centered way. He had sustained me as well, though he would probably never know how much.

EPILOGUE

CHARLIE GRADUATED from college with a degree in government. He continues to live in Texas. Nia lives with him. Her photo, the one on James' business card, now graces some of Starmark Academy's training tools in local pet stores.

James went on to become a top trainer at the academy. He has two dogs of his own.

Grant joined him in working at the academy. A talented mechanic in all things, he now maintains the facilities. He has two therapy dogs.

Sarah graduated from college with a degree in psychology. She has an interest in improving the lives of veterans.

I eventually moved to Texas and took a job at an animal hospital. The daily human interaction is good for me. Animals offer a connection with humans.

I know this to be true.